The DIVINE ATTRACTION

The DIVINE ATTRACTION

The Power of Intimate Worship

A GOD WORKING WITH GOD BOOK

WARREN HUNTER

DESTINY IMAGE® PUBLISHERS, INC.
P.O. Box 310, Shippensburg, PA 17257-0310

"Speaking to the Purposes of God for This Generation
and for the Generations to Come."

This book and all other Destiny Image, Revival Press, Mercy Place, Fresh Bread, Destiny Image Fiction, and Treasure House books are available at Christian bookstores and distributors worldwide.

For a U.S. bookstore nearest you, call 1-800-722-6774.

For more information on foreign distributors, call 717-532-3040.

Reach us on the Internet: www.destinyimage.com.

ISBN 10: 0-7684-2713-4

ISBN 13: 978-0-7684-2713-4

For Worldwide Distribution, Printed in the U.S.A.

1 2 3 4 5 6 7 8 9 10 11 / 12 11 10 09 08

CONTENTS

CHAPTER ONE

LOVE'S ROOTS

Behold what manner of love the Father has bestowed
on us, that we should be called children of God!
(1 John 3:1a)

All people in every nation across every continent in the world were fashioned to do one thing primarily: that is, to love the Lord their God with all of their heart, soul, mind, and strength. God has called us to love Him without holding anything back, with complete abandonment to His great love, freely worshiping Him as He really is. For this reason I was created, and for this same reason you were created. God desires that every person alive should love Him with singleness of heart. The perhaps disconcerting truth, however, is that we cannot love Him. No, in and of ourselves we do not have the ability to love God as He really is, offering Him the true love and worship that He desires and is so worthy of. In fact there have only been two men in the history of all mankind who were ever able to offer God perfect worship. The first was Adam, before the Fall. Adam was created just like God: perfect in every way. Adam could love and worship God with complete purity and abandonment to God's love. When Adam fell, however, he stripped himself of this ability. The inevitable consequence of Adam's choice to sin was that his God-given and God-like nature was traded for the nature of the father of lies, namely, satan. Adam chose to hand over his God-given ability to worship God in spirit and truth. Now man does not innately have the ability to love and worship God or to fulfill God's greatest desire, which is to see His own nature and character reflected back to Him.

Discouraging as this beginning might seem, do not be alarmed. This ability to love and worship God was restored by the last Adam, Jesus Christ. Although Adam sinned and volitionally gave up his ability to love God, Jesus came to the earth, volitionally giving up His heavenly throne, so that man could be restored to righteous relationship with God through His death and resurrection. In order to know God's love in its deepest sense, we must understand that it is Jesus' blood that makes a way into the throne room of God for all people. God's love is the foundational truth of all Scripture, and the cross of Jesus Christ is the foundational demonstration of that love.

As God's children, believers in the Word of God, we must come to grips with the truth that God is not looking for anything of human origin. He is not interested in what we as humans can give Him. We breathe due to an act of His mercy. We can walk and talk and live because of His grace. In fact, all creation is living off the overflow of God's covenant relationship with Himself which He established through the cross and resurrection of His Son Jesus Christ. God is not attracted to mere human praise and worship. God does not enjoy listening to songs—in fact God does not need or pursue the musical expressions of human beings at all! Brothers and sisters, understand me clearly: God jealously desires Himself, nothing more and nothing less. God is at this present time going to and fro over the face of the earth looking for a heart like His—a loyal heart, a heart that is blameless before Him (see 2 Chron. 16:9). He is not looking for human talent, wisdom, understanding, or love.

> For the message of the cross is foolishness to those who are perishing, but to us who are being saved it is the power of God. For it is written: "I will destroy the wisdom of the wise, and bring to nothing the understanding of the prudent." Where is the wise? Where is the scribe? Where is the disputer of this age? Has not God made foolish the wisdom of this world? For since, in the wisdom of God, the world through wisdom did not know God, it pleased God through the foolishness of the message preached to save those who believe.... Because the foolishness of God is wiser

than men, and the weakness of God is stronger than
men (1 Corinthians 1:18-21,25).

It is only when God hears Himself proceeding out of the hearts of believers that God is attracted to our love and worship. You see, God is not impressed by us. God is only impressed by Himself. God only promotes Himself. God is only attracted to Himself. God only works with what He finds of Himself within us. The key to understanding our love relationship with God is to know that it is only the Holy Spirit within us, who is God, who can love God properly, according to the Spirit, and give God back the love and worship He deserves. God loves what is of God. Once we understand this principle it is clear that God's love is the very center and core of worship. In fact worship is an exchange of God's love to us and God's love through us. God loves everything that has its seed or origin in God. It was through the seeds of deception that satan sowed his influence which resulted in the Fall of man; but it is through the seeds of God's grace (His loving divine influence) that what belongs to God can be restored and redeemed to its original place as the belonging of God. It is the reflection and influence of this redemptive, restorative process of God's love manifesting through us that multiplies the God loving God relationship within us. Throughout the pages of this book, we will discuss what God's role is in our intimate relationship with Him and what our role is as the ones who are receiving His love. Get ready to be touched by the very essence of God's being: His love!

LOVE'S FIRST BREATH

In the beginning was the Word, and the Word was with God, and the Word was God. He was in the beginning with God. All things were made through Him, and without Him nothing was made that was made. In Him [the Word, God] *was life, and the life was the light of men* (John 1:1-4).

In the beginning, before God created the earth and all that is on it, God was face to face with God. Before God said, "Let there be light," God was already in intimate communication with Himself, loving Himself, and having perfect relationship with Himself. The above passage tells us that before God started to create anything, the Word, which is God, was "with" God. In the English language, the word *with* has very little significance. *With* is a common word and can be used in many contexts. English speakers the world over use this word hundreds of times every day without giving the word and its meaning a second thought. Due to the flippant way we view our own language, it can be easy to read over a passage of Scripture and miss a very important aspect of the revelation that God wants us to glean from it. In the Greek, the word which we translate as *with* is *pros. Pros*, according to *Strong's Exhaustive Concordance of the Bible*, means "towards, in the front of, face to face."[1] In English, if a person states, "I attended a church service with Sister Smith— ," we do not assume that the two people stood face to face during the service. They could have been sitting next to each other or merely have driven together. Yet in the Greek, when John wrote, "the Word was with God," he meant to imply that God was face to face with God. He was drawing a picture of nearness and intimacy in which the two were standing in such close proximity that They were touching. We see within the Godhead perfect love demonstrated: God loving God.

As we discussed in the first volume of *God Working With God*, the writers of the New Testament were all Jewish, and it is important, when studying the Greek, to look at the parallel Hebrew word or words and their meaning. The intimacy demonstrated by the Greek word *pros* is also found in the Hebrew word *al-peney*. According to Doug Wheeler, a Hebrew scholar and professor, *al-peney* means "to turn oneself, to turn towards and to face, to be in the front or forepart. It also means to be face to face and in the presence of."[2] As the Spirit of God hovered over the waters of the deep in Genesis chapter 1, the Spirit of God was face to face with the dark waters, hovering and brooding over them as a mother eagle broods over her nest. This is a beautiful picture of love and intimacy which is painted for us at the very beginning of Scripture. In order to create all things, God's Spirit lovingly cherished and brooded over God's creation waiting for God's Word to be spoken. When God's Word went forth, "Let there be light," the Spirit of God went to work with the Word of God, and the first act of intimacy recorded in the Bible took place. You see, the Word of God was face to face with the Spirit of God.

Beloved, let us love one another, for love is of God; and everyone who loves is born of God and knows God. He who does not love does not know God, for God is love (1 John 4:7-8).

It is most imperative that we grasp how important God's love is. All things that were created are a product of God's love relationship with Himself. At the moment that God spoke His Word over creation, the Spirit of God went to work with the Word of God. The two had intimate communication and relationship, and from that place of intimacy, the creation was birthed. The Spirit of God was face to face with the Word of God, and the Word of God created and formed all flesh. (See John 1:14.)

Intimacy is the birthplace of miracles.

It is not possible to separate love from worship or worship from love. The two are intertwined like the cords that make up a strong rope. Remember love is God. Many think of love as merely an attribute of God, or part of God's character. Yet, the Bible makes it clear that love is more than just a part of God—it is God's essence. God is love! There is no other aspect of God which is made equal to Him in definition. Here is a fresh way of looking at John 1:1 that will shed light on the power of God's love: "In the beginning was Love; and Love was face to face with Love, and Love was Love!" We could also say, "In the beginning was God; and God was face to face with God, and God was God." Let's look at a few Scriptures that show us how God and His love are woven together so that the two cannot be separated.

> *I love those who love Me, and those who seek Me diligently will find Me* (Proverbs 8:17).

> *But if anyone loves God, this one is known by Him* (1 Corinthians 8:3).

> *Blessed be the God and Father of our Lord Jesus Christ, who has blessed us with every spiritual blessing in heavenly places in Christ, just as He chose us in Him before the foundation of the world, that we should be holy and without blame before Him in love, having predestined us to adoption as sons by Jesus Christ to Himself, according to the good pleasure of His will* (Ephesians 1:3-5).

Do you realize that before time began, God had a love plan for you? Love predestined you to be holy and without blame before Him in love.

TAKE ME BACK TO EDEN

In the beginning, God created the heavens and the earth. The

Book of Revelation, chapter 4, verse 11, tells us that all things were created for God's pleasure (KJV). It is important to understand what brings God pleasure when we set our minds to worship Him. God did not create the earth merely for man to enjoy, though we too benefit from and enjoy creation. The plants and the animals, the sun, moon, and stars were all created to delight God's heart. Man was the crown of God's creation, the pinnacle of His creative work; therefore, man was called to bring God the most pleasure. Man was called to be one with God. And as man was one with God, man was allowed the privilege of sharing in God's pleasure. So much so, that God created a special place for man to dwell in. This place was called the Garden of Eden. This garden was no ordinary place; it was an oasis of fertile plants. Fruit trees of every sort grew there, including the Tree of Life, which, if one ate of its fruit, would give that person eternal life.

Eden was a place where animals lived peacefully with one another and were enjoyed by the man and woman. Both men and animals ate vegetables and fruits. Eden was a place surrounded by gold and gems. Even the ground itself was full of valuable treasures. In Eden there was a garden which was brimming with natural glory. God created a place of natural glory in order to usher in the presence of supernatural glory: It was in Eden that God walked and talked with man. God created an environment that was conducive to His presence and power.

The environment found in Eden was the environment of the spirit. God's heavenly environment dwelt on earth in the Garden of Eden. Even the word *Eden* in Hebrew means "pleasure, pleasant, to be soft, to live voluptuously."[3] What a wonderful word to describe the heavenly environment of the spirit. God wanted Adam to live in an environment of both natural and supernatural glory. God did not create man to live in a fallen, corrupted, and accursed world. He created a world that was in order with His own nature and character. To take man out of this environment would be similar to taking a fish out of water: it flops around, moves, and wiggles, yet accomplishes nothing. However, if the fish is thrown back into the water, it immediately can swim and move as fast as it wants. The fish's environment now fits its makeup. We have already established that God can only work with what is of God's nature and character. The Bible teaches us that man was the exact image of God. The implication of this truth is that the man of God, namely Adam, would only be able to function within an environment that perfectly reflected God's nature. Adam would only be able to work with what was of God, just as God only worked with what was of God.

Man was created to live in this spiritual environment. Many people say, "One day, when I get to Heaven, I'll see Jesus," or they will say, "One day when we get to Heaven we'll know the truth." These statements do not line up with the purposes of God. God desires for His children to draw near to Him right now. His Word promises that if we will seek God, we will find Him, for He is not far away, no matter where we are. Jesus came to reestablish the Kingdom of Heaven on earth: Jesus died in order that man would once again perfectly reflect who God is and live within an environment that is conducive to God's voice, presence, and power.

> *For thus says the High and Lofty One who inhabits eternity, whose name is Holy: "I dwell in the high and holy place, with him who has a contrite and humble spirit, to revive the spirit of the humble, and to revive the heart of the contrite ones"* (Isaiah 57:15).

> *For I know the thoughts that I think toward you, says the Lord, thoughts of peace and not of evil, to give you a future and a hope. Then you will call upon Me and go and pray to Me, and I will listen to you. And you will seek Me and find Me, when you search for Me with all your heart. I will be found by you, says the Lord, and I will bring you back from your captivity; I will gather you from all the nations and from all the places where I have driven you, says the Lord, and I will bring you to the place from which I cause you to be carried away captive* (Jeremiah 29:11-14).

> *And He has made from one blood every nation of men to dwell on all the face of the earth, and has determined their preappointed times and the boundaries of their dwellings, so that they should seek the Lord, in the hope that they might grope for Him and*

find Him, though He is not far from each one of us;
for in Him we live and move and have our being, as
also some of your own poets have said, "For we are
also His offspring" (Acts 17:26-28).

Therefore submit to God. Resist the devil and he will
flee from you. Draw near to God and He will draw near
to you. Cleanse your hands, you sinners; and purify
your hearts, you double-minded (James 4:7-8).

When we worship and praise God, we need to understand that we are releasing God's nature and character before God and toward God. By doing this we are reestablishing the environment of the spirit. The Bible teaches us that God inhabits the praises of His people. If we believe the Word of God is true, then we should expect God to show up in power every time we praise Him! If we will allow our expectation to line up with the Word of God, we will see that God has never once failed to perform His Word. Worship creates an environment, so that who we are according to God's Word in the Spirit is what we manifest in the natural. God wants to bring forth His best, the fullness of the Godhead bodily. Paul told the Galatians that he labored in birth pangs that Christ would be formed in them (see Gal. 4:19). God wants to birth Christ in our lives so that we can experience the fullness of what He has for us. God desires to draw us back into Eden, back into the place of perfect worship of His majesty and perfect union with His being.

Worship is releasing God's nature and character before God and toward God.

THE BLESSING OF GOD

Did you know that the first words Adam's ears ever heard were blessing? Yes, the first words which God spoke over Adam were words of blessing. The words that opened Adam's ears, the first communication that took place between God and Adam was blessing. Remember that God created Adam from the dust of the ground, in His own image and likeness. God designed Adam to be just like God in every respect.

> *Then God said, "Let Us make man in Our image, according to Our likeness; let them have dominion over the fish of the sea, over the birds of the air, and over the cattle, over all the earth and over every creeping thing that creeps on the earth." So God created man in His own image; in the image of God He created him; male and female He created them* (Genesis 1:26-27).

What I want to make clear here is that God initiated blessing. God can and will only bless God. This is a key principle to understanding the reciprocal nature of God. God is the One who is blessed in and of Himself; He has always been blessed because He is the beginning of all good things. Anything that is good in the physical, soulical, or spiritual realms proceeded out of God alone. In other words, blessing cannot be initiated by man. God has been proclaiming blessing over His people forever. He is blessed and the blessing; it is only when we receive the blessing of God that we can return blessing. When we receive God's blessing and release it back to God verbally, God reciprocates with more blessings—this is how God in Heaven blesses what is of God in His children. God spoke blessing over Adam because he was the very same as God in every way except for the fact that he was created under God's supervision and after God's order, to be a partaker of God's divine nature. Therefore, God blessed God's nature. Because we are created in the similitude of God, this same nature has been written in our hearts. When Adam was first created, he had the ability to bless in a perfect fashion; he learned this from his Father. And, of course, when Eve was created, Adam immediately spoke blessing over her.

> And Adam said: "This is now bone of my bones and
> flesh of my flesh. She shall be called Woman, because
> she was taken out of Man" (Genesis 2:23).

When Adam chose to sin against God, he was really choosing to give up the identity, DNA, and nature which he had received from God for another identity, DNA, and nature—that of the devil. Adam rejected his Father, and when he rejected his Father, he was choosing to have another father—namely, satan. Now instead of blessing, Adam was subject to the curse; instead of truth, Adam was subject to deception; instead of love, Adam was subject to fear.

The power of the cross is that Jesus has now restored this relationship. He came as both God and man and reconciled man to God.

> **The first Adam's choice to be fatherless was overturned by the last Adam's choice to be obedient to His Father, even unto death.**

Now, man's position as God's image bearer has been restored through Jesus Christ. Those who believe in Jesus trade in the old man for the new. They reject the curse to live the blessing; they reject the deception to live the truth; they reject fear to live love.

Through the redemptive work of Jesus Christ, we see that our ability to bless God and to bless others has been restored. Even under the Old Covenant, those who walked and talked with God had the ability (because of divine relationship) to bless their sons:

> *And Abraham gave all that he had to Isaac. But Abraham gave gifts to the sons of the concubines which Abraham had; and while he was still living he sent them eastward, away from Isaac his son, to the country of the east* (Genesis 25:5-6).

And he came near and kissed him; and he smelled the smell of his clothing, and blessed him and said: "Surely, the smell of my son is like the smell of a field which the Lord has blessed. Therefore may God give you of the dew of heaven, of the fatness of the earth, and plenty of grain and wine. Let peoples serve you, and nations bow down to you. Be master over your brethren, and let your mother's sons bow down to you. Cursed be everyone who curses you, and blessed be those who bless you!" (Genesis 27:27-29)

Then Isaac called Jacob and blessed him, and charged him, and said to him: "You shall not take a wife from the daughters of Canaan. Arise, go to Padan Aram, to the house of Bethuel your mother's father; and take yourself a wife from there of the daughters of Laban your mother's brother. May God Almighty bless you, and make you fruitful and multiply you, that you may be an assembly of peoples; and give you the blessing of Abraham, to you and your descendants with you, that you may inherit the land in which you are a stranger, which God gave to Abraham" (Genesis 28:1-4).

And he blessed Joseph, and said: "God, before whom

*my fathers Abraham and Isaac walked, the God who
has fed me all my life long to this day, the Angel who
has redeemed me from all evil, bless the lads; let my
name be named upon them, and the name of my
fathers Abraham and Isaac; and let them grow into
a multitude in the midst of the earth"* (Genesis
48:15-16).

In the above verses, we see the patriarchs of our faith blessing
their sons. Each man's blessing enabled the son of that man to prosper in greater measure than his father. Jacob confessed this in verse
26 of Genesis chapter 49: "The blessings of your father have excelled
the blessings of my ancestors, up to the utmost bound of the everlasting hills…." Due to their covenant with God, they were able to
step into part of their identities as image bearers of God. Through
covenant, God was beginning to restore what was lost through
Adam's sin.

As man was blessed by God, man was able also to bless God.
We see this demonstrated very strongly in the psalms of David. In
24 different verses, David is either blessing God or instructing his
soul or others to bless the Lord. First Samuel 13:13-15 tells us that
David was a man after God's own heart. Here we see this attribute
of God's nature and character extended from David toward God.
Expressing and declaring blessing over God was a very important
part of Old Covenant worship, and was carried out through the
lives of the patriarchs until the carrying away of Judah to Babylon.

When temple worship was reinstated under the rule of Cyrus the Persian, speaking verbal blessing over God and over His people was still a normal part of worship:

> *And he blessed him and said: "Blessed be Abram of God Most High, Possessor of heaven and earth; and blessed be God Most High, who has delivered your enemies into your hand"* (Genesis 14:19-20).

> *Then the man bowed down his head and worshiped the Lord. And he said, "Blessed be the Lord God of my master Abraham, who has not forsaken His mercy and His truth toward my master..."* (Genesis 24:26-27).

> *Then the women said to Naomi, "Blessed be the Lord, who has not left you this day without a close relative; and may his name be famous in Israel!"* (Ruth 4:14)

> *The David said to Abigail: "Blessed is the Lord God of Israel, who sent you this day to meet me! And blessed is your advice and blessed are you, because you have kept me this day from coming to bloodshed and from avenging myself with my own hand"* (1 Samuel 25:32-33).

Blessed be the Lord God of Israel from everlasting to everlasting! And all the people said, "Amen!" and praised the Lord (1 Chronicles 16:36).

"Blessed be the Lord God of our fathers, who has put such a thing as this in the king's heart, to beautify the house of the Lord which is in Jerusalem (Ezra 7:27).

And Ezra blessed the Lord, the great God. Then all the people answered, "Amen, Amen!" while lifting up their hands. And they bowed their heads and worshiped the Lord with their faces to the ground (Nehemiah 8:6).

This trend we see through the Old Covenant Scriptures is carried over into the New Covenant by Jesus. Jesus spoke verbal blessing over His disciples a total of 14 times in the book of Matthew alone. In comparison, there is only one time mentioned in Matthew where people blessed Jesus. It occurs in chapter 21, verse 9:

Then the multitude who went before and those who followed cried out, saying: "Hosanna to the Son of David! 'Blessed is He who comes in the name of the Lord!' Hosanna in the highest!"

Of course, their words proved shallow: the crowd that wanted to make Jesus king that day was unified in the purpose of crucifying Him three days later. Yet Jesus told the disciples, "Most assuredly, I say to you, he who believes in Me, the works that I do he will do also; and greater works than these he will do, because I go to My Father" (John 14:12). Again Jesus is imparting to the disciples the ability to speak blessing.

> *God has called us to receive His blessing and*
> *to be a blessing to God and to others.*

The great apostle Paul began all of his letters but one (Galatians) with thanking God or blessing God. It is as if Paul is saying, "You have blessed me, therefore I will bless you." Immediately, you see that Paul is not merely writing to reach and minister to people. He is writing first and foremost as an act of blessing and worship toward God. As Paul contends in Galatians 1:10, "For do I now persuade men, or God? Or do I seek to please men? For if I still pleased men, I would not be a bondservant of Christ." Paul wants us to understand that he cares nothing for the opinion of man. Paul wants to please, bless, and worship God through his message. This is a principle that I teach leaders in the churches wherever I go:

> *Learn to worship God with your message.*

This is a very simple concept. If you are a pastor of a church, you may give two or three sermons a week. Sometimes, people will really enjoy your messages. They will approach you after service and confess, "Pastor, your message really touched me today." Or they might say, "Wow, Pastor! That was a great message. It really filled me up." It is obvious that these people are focused on themselves when they come to hear the message. On the other hand, if the message was correction, it may be that no one will approach you after the service; if the message was really convicting, people may even leave your church! But take heart: when you walk out of a meeting, the opinion of your Father God is the only one that should carry weight. If you communicated the message He wanted you to, you were offering your Father acceptable worship, a sweet-smelling fragrance in His nostrils. If the Holy Spirit rises up in you and says, "Well done, good and faithful servant," that is the only praise that matters. As ministers we must allow the voice of God to silence the voices of human opinion, which the enemy sends our way to distract us.

In every situation we face, we must make worshiping God our focus. When you walk away from any circumstance, your goal should be to hear God say, "You did well!" Remember that God is moved by His nature. That means any time you demonstrate the nature and character of God, it is an act of worship to the Father. If you bless those who curse you, you are acting as Jesus did, and with this behavior God is well pleased.

In order to bless, brothers and sisters, we must open our mouths. We have to be willing to speak that blessing! Remember that God's breath propels His word. When man was created, God breathed into him the breath of life. God's breath now resides within every believer and must be released to propel God's word into every atmosphere. God is not interested in our words, our feelings, our selfish desires. He is listening for the sound of His Spirit to be released through our mouths. When we do this, the words we speak will carry weight in the spirit realm and will accomplish God's purposes![4]

WHOM DO YOU HONOR?

There is a place in worship where we begin to tap into the honor that God deserves. The Bible teaches us that God honors those who honor Him, and that promotion only comes to those who honor God. There has been much study on the person called Jabez in the Bible. His prayer to God is usually the focus of people's study. Yet I see a "God working with God" connection within the short story of this man. Before God answered his prayer there is a statement made about his character: namely, that "Jabez was more honorable than his brothers" (1 Chron. 4:9). God blessed this man because He discovered something of Himself worth promoting: His honor.

You may be wondering why certain things in your life are not moving forward. Where is the long-awaited breakthrough you believe God has promised? First Samuel 2:30 tells us that God honors those who honor Him. It could be that there are some areas of your heart where you are not honoring God. There have been many times when I have had people come to me with difficult financial situations. They tell me they do not have enough money to pay the bills, let alone save for the future. My first question to them is, "Have you been honoring God with your finances?" This offends some people. Yet we must be willing to receive correction from God's Word if we are hungry for change.

> *Honor the Lord with your possessions, and with the firstfruits of all your increase; so your barns will be filled with plenty, and your vats will overflow with new wine* (Proverbs 3:9-10).

If we are willing to honor God, we will find that He will honor us. It is when we withhold from God what is due Him, that we find ourselves in want. The area may not be finances in your life. It may be spending time with the Lord every day, reading the Word, or praying for your leaders. It may be in the area of godly priorities. Whatever it is, we need to be willing to change our behavior. Then we will see God begin to honor us.

We need to create an environment that is so attractive to God's nature and character that He feels welcome in our lives, homes, and work places. God will not "show up and show off" for us if the environment we create is full of bitterness, strife, and disorder. God will not honor an environment that is not full of honor and love. All of this is connected to the attitudes we emanate.

The attitude that you exude is the signature of your life.

Our attitude will either attract God or repel Him; our attitude will either attract His blessings or repel them; our attitude will either attract acceptance and breakthrough or repel them. Our attitude is a fragrance and a color that we are releasing from our body that will either draw the divine presence toward us or repel Him away from us.

The genuine love, honor, and fire of God will attract even those who do not know God. The world is constantly trying to counterfeit what we have in the Kingdom of God. They are trying so hard to have what we have without stepping into the Kingdom; when they see the genuineness of the Spirit of God, they will be attracted even if they do not want to be. When you leave the church building after a service, and even every morning after you have spent time with the Father, you should be emanating the love and joy of God. You should feel fire for the lost. You should feel desire for all of God and none of you. And if this is the case with you, don't be surprised when God begins to honor you! He is going to and fro over the earth looking for a heart that is like His (see 2 Chron. 16:9); when He finds you walking out the honor of God in your everyday life, and in every aspect of your life, He will open the windows of Heaven to honor and bless you.

> *As we honor God for who He is and what He has done in our lives, we make room for God to work through us and in us on a daily basis.*

In the Hebrew culture all actions were considered worship of some sort. In the Book of Leviticus, God specifically instructs the Levites on every area of life, even how and when to relieve themselves. They were anointed to minister before God in the tabernacle and their every action was calculated to please God and to offer worship to God. Their actions were either worship of God the Creator or worship of a false god. The attitudes of a person depicted who and what they worshiped. Even simple things like the ability to eat or to use the restroom were considered worship! The Hebrews believed that they should be thankful for every part of their lives and worship with every action they performed. If they were able to sit down to have a meal, they should be thankful and offer up worship to God. They believed that to worship God a person must honor him in every aspect of his or her life. A person could not claim to love YHWH and offer sacrifices at a pagan temple; in the same way, a person could not claim to love YHWH and grumble and complain, or mistreat his family. Thankfulness was an integral part of their lives because they wanted to demonstrate their love for God at every moment of their lives. If a person showed respect and reverence to another person, it was considered worship, a demonstration of their love for God. To study the Word was considered the highest form of worship. This powerful concept is perpetuated in the New Testament by the apostle Paul in the book of Romans:

> *I beseech you therefore, brethren, by the mercies of*
> *God, that you present your bodies a living sacrifice,*
> *holy, acceptable unto God, which is your reasonable*

service. And be not conformed to this world, but be transformed by the renewing of your mind, that you may prove what is that good and acceptable and perfect will of God (Romans 12:1-2).

Everything that we do is considered worship to God. He does not merely desire our spirits to be one with Him—God also wants our souls (our mind, will, and emotions) and our bodies. Everything we do is to be consecrated to Him. God wants a living sacrifice, holy and acceptable. He wants us to prove what is the good, acceptable, and perfect will of God. It is through the renewing of our minds that we come to the place where we can do just that— recognize God's will and move from glory to glory as we become His will. How do we renew our minds? Our minds will be truly transformed when we meditate on God's Word, study it, understand it, accept it, and keep it.

God honors the place of original revelation and intimacy.

To study the Word takes a great expenditure of time, energy, and resources. If a person truly wants to hear from God, he or she will have to give hours to Bible study and study materials. God sees this offering of time as worship and honors the place where original revelation and intimacy is birthed. The reason God's honor is attracted to the place of origination is because it demonstrates God's own creative nature. God loves to see us birthing new revelation, something straight from His mind that no one has ever known before. To demonstrate God's love through acts of worship was the most important part of a Hebrew person's life. The importance of studying the Word of God takes us back to the reciprocal nature of God. As I have stated in the first volume of *God Working With God: To the degree that you value the Word, respect the Word, esteem the Word, exalt the Word, and honor the Word, to that degree that Word works in your life.*

When we honor God's Word, God will honor us. In this way we are loving and worshiping God by bowing down to the Word of God. Again, the concept of honoring God's Word is wrapped in the nature of God's love. It is impossible to honor God's Word without loving and worshiping God. Jesus said, "You shall know the truth, and the truth shall make you free" (John 8:32). In the Hebrew culture, to "know" something or someone was to be intimately acquainted with that thing or person. If a man "knew" his wife, he knew her in a spiritually, soulically, and physically intimate way.

> *Then Joseph being raised from sleep did as the angel of the Lord had bidden him, and took unto him his wife: and knew her not till she had brought forth her firstborn son: and he called His name Jesus* (Matthew 1:24-25 KJV).

You see, God wants us to be intimately acquainted with the truth; as Jesus said in John 14:6, "I am the way, the truth, and the life." If we are intimately acquainted with the Word, we will be able to worship God as He really is, offering Him the true worship that He wants: "God is Spirit, and those who worship Him must worship in spirit and truth" (John 4:24). Remember, as a child of God, you are called to find your identity in the Word of God. Even Jesus did this when He quoted Isaiah 61:1-2 in the synagogue early in His ministry: "The Spirit of the Lord is upon Me, because He has anointed Me to preach the gospel to the poor; He has sent me to heal the brokenhearted, to proclaim liberty to the captives and recovery of sight to the blind, to set at liberty those who are oppressed; to proclaim the acceptable year of the Lord" (Luke 4:18-19). Jesus was saying, in essence, "I am who the Word says I am, because I am the Word become flesh." This is the same claim that we as God's children can make today. You are a word from the Word. You were given purpose and grace in Him before time began (see 2 Tim. 1:9). You must worship God by studying and becoming intimately acquainted with God's Word—not only because you will find out who God is, but because you will find out who God wants to be in you! Your identity as God's image bearer is found in the Word, just as Jesus' identity was.[5]

THE BIGGEST LOVERS ARE THE BIGGEST GIVERS

So far, we have seen how love and honor play an integral role in true worship of God. All of the areas touched on in this first chapter will be discussed in greater detail further on in the book; right now we are just warming up with an overview of the important aspects of our role as worshipers of God. Remember, all of the different aspects of worship are wrapped up in the principle of "God working with God." God in Heaven works with God in us to bring forth what is of God. This is how true worship is birthed: when God touches God, God's love will manifest.

Another element that becomes a powerful factor in worship is sacrifice. It can be a simple thing at times to come before the Father and tell him, "I love You, Lord." However, our love is laid on the line when God asks us to place something of value to us on His altar. That is, of course, exactly what He asks us to do with everything that belongs to us. Paul makes it clear in Philippians 3:10-11 that in order for us to attain the resurrection of the dead, we must know Him in "the fellowship of His sufferings, being conformed to His death." Jesus tells us in Matthew 16:25, "Whoever desires to save his life will lose it, but whoever loses his life for My sake will find it." God is looking for living sacrifices, men and women who are willing to "count all things loss for the excellence" of knowing Him (Phil. 3:7-8).

You can give without loving, but you cannot love without giving.

In John 3:16, Jesus tells Nicodemus that "God so loved the world that He gave...." God's own love compelled Him to give. And what did God give? He gave Himself. This is what God expects of us; this is true worship. We see this love demonstrated again by the Son when He says to the Pharisees, "I speak what I have seen with My Father" (John 8:38). It is easy to see that it was love for the Father that compelled Jesus to lay down His own life on the cross. God demonstrated His great love by sacrificing, and we are called to manifest God's nature toward God by demonstrating sacrifice and servanthood for the call of God to go into all the world.

When it comes to worshiping God in a way that pleases Him, we must remember the importance of God's reciprocal nature. This is dealt with in detail in the first chapter of *God Working With God*, volume one; we will only give a summary here. Remember, if you give, it will be given unto you. If you forgive, it will be forgiven you. If you do not forgive, it will not be forgiven you. If you honor God, He will honor you. If you draw near to God, God will draw near to you. If you reject the Word, God will reject you. If you show mercy, you will reap mercy. It is important to note that the key to tapping into God's forgiveness is to forgive. The key to reaping mercy is to show mercy. The key to receiving honor is to honor God. This reciprocal principle applies to every aspect of God's nature and character. At this point, it becomes clear that the quickest way to access God's nature is to demonstrate God's nature to Him. Of course, we are still growing in our ability to manifest the character of God; however, God will respond whether we exhibit His nature to a small or large degree.

We may understand the reciprocal nature of God's dealings

with us best when we recognize the high value God places on covenant. For example, under the Old Covenant, mercy was only shown to those who were in covenant relationship with God. This meant that God would show them His *checed*. This Hebrew word actually means God's steadfast covenant love and devotion. If a person showed mercy to another person, that person was actually showering the receiver with the blessings of covenant. Mercy was wrapped with love and reminded God of His own promise to be loving, devoted, and merciful to those who were in covenant with Him. The concept of *checed* will be covered in more detail in chapter four. I mention it now so that you can see the connection between showing mercy and God's reciprocal nature. When we give sacrificially to God, we are bringing to God's remembrance His own sacrificial nature and the great sacrifice He made by sending Jesus to the cross. In the same way, when we are merciful, we are putting God in remembrance of His covenant promises which He has established with us. When we put God in remembrance of Himself, we can expect God's response. God is righteous, and He loves those who are righteous. God is looking for God, and when He finds Himself, He will respond.

Let me reiterate that God is not impressed with good works unless those works are wrapped in His nature and character. We see a good example of this if we compare King Saul to King David. First Samuel 9:2 tells us that Saul was a man of great stature. Many people were impressed by who he was on the outside. Yet God is not impressed by what impresses humans. First Samuel 15:17 tells us that it was when Saul was little in his own eyes that God made him the king over all of Israel. God did not make Saul king because of what he had accomplished, but because he was humble. Over time, however, Saul became great in his own eyes and even set up a monument to himself instead of giving God the glory for the victories won.

> *So when Samuel rose early in the morning to meet Saul, it was told Samuel, saying, "Saul went to Carmel, and indeed, he set up a monument for himself; and he has gone on around, passed by, and gone down to Gilgal" (1 Samuel 15:12).*

Saul chose to listen to the voice of the people, instead of obeying God's voice. When we listen to the whispering of others, it brings a curse on our lives.

> *And Saul said to Samuel, "But I have obeyed the voice of the Lord, and gone on the mission on which the Lord sent me, and brought back Agag king of Amalek; I have utterly destroyed the Amalekites. But the people took of the plunder, sheep and oxen, the best of the things which should have been utterly destroyed, to sacrifice to the Lord your God in Gilgal" (1 Samuel 15:20-21).*

Even though Saul defeated the Amalekites and brought back

animals to sacrifice to the Lord, God was not impressed. The Lord wanted obedience, not sacrifice. In contrast, the young David was not a mighty warrior, though he had been proved by killing a lion and a bear. He did not fight battles, and when the time came for the Israelites to go to war against the Philistines, David's brothers left him behind to tend the sheep. David was a mere shepherd boy who wrote songs to the Lord, yet God was more impressed by the love that He found in David than with all of Saul's conquests. Do you remember what God told Samuel when the Lord sent the prophet to anoint a new king over Israel?

> So it was, when they came, that he looked at Eliab and said, "Surely the Lord's anointed is before Him!" But the Lord said to Samuel, "Do not look at his appearance or at his physical stature, because I have refused him. For the Lord does not see as man sees; for man looks at the outward appearance, but the Lord looks at the heart" (1 Samuel 16:6-7).

When we do "good works" we need to remember that God is looking at our hearts to see whether our works are birthed out of the right attitude. God wants to know if we are really serving and giving out of a pure heart; a pure heart is attractive to God because it is a heart like His. Is our sacrifice wrapped in the nature and character of God, or are we giving out of obligation, bitterness, fear, etc? God will only respond to God. That is why Samuel told Saul, "But now your kingdom shall not continue. The Lord has sought for Himself a man after His own heart, and the Lord has commanded him to be commander over His people, because you have not kept what the Lord commanded you" (1 Sam. 13:14).

Saul lost his right to be the leader over God's covenant people because he did not manifest God's covenant principles.

God knows how to give His life for us. Through the act of giving His Son as a sacrifice, God was demonstrating to us how we are to give love back to Him. In the same way, Jesus demonstrated for us how we are to love one another. God has never asked us to do anything which He has not already done Himself. In John 13, Jesus washed the feet of His disciples. In verses 12 through 17, He tells them:

> *Do you know what I have done to you? You call Me Teacher and Lord, and you say well, for so I am. If I then, your Lord and Teacher, have washed your feet, you also ought to wash one another's feet. For I have given you an example, that you should do as I have done to you. Most assuredly, I say to you, a servant is not greater than his master; nor is he who is sent greater than he who sent him. If you know these things, blessed are you if you do them.*

Even though Jesus was God, He stood among His disciples as a servant in order to be the master copy of what they should be. Though we are kings and priests and will judge the earth one day (see 1 Cor. 6:2), we are called to be the servants of all. It is clear that Jesus could not have been King of kings and Lord of lords had He not first "humbled Himself and became obedient to the point of death" (Phil. 2:8). God is a faithful and true witness to God. In fact, God is the only consistently faithful and true witness to God. Therefore, the only way we as believers will be able to take on this image of humility and authority is to allow God's nature to work in and through us.

> *Grace and peace be multiplied to you in the knowledge of God and of Jesus our Lord, as His divine power has given to us all things that pertain to life and godliness, through the knowledge of Him who called us by glory and virtue, by which have been given to us exceedingly great and precious promises, that through these you may be partakers of the divine nature, having escaped the corruption that is in the world through lust (2 Peter 1:2-4).*

The apostle Peter uses a very interesting Greek word in verse 4. The word, which has been translated here as *partakers*, is actually the Greek word *koinonos*, which means associate or partner.[6] God wants you to become an associate, a partner in His nature so that

41

you can escape the corruption that is in the world through lust. *Koinonos* is a very strong word; it means to have in common. Peter is telling us that we no longer have anything in common with the world which is full of the corruption of lust. Instead, we have one nature in common with God—it is a divine, spotless, and death-less nature, which the apostle also talks about in his first epistle (see 1 Pet. 1:15-25).

HOW BIG IS GOD?

It is important to recognize that the fullness of the Godhead is within you bodily. Colossians 1:27 tells us that Christ in us is the hope of glory. What is God's glory? In the Greek, the word that we translate as *glory* is the word *doxa*.[7] According to *Strong's Concordance, doxa* is all that God is and all that He does, manifested in and through the believer. God desires for all of His nature and character to be manifest in and through His children. Yet if we do not believe in God's bigness and are not convinced of His power, we will not see the fullness of who He is manifesting in our lives. You see, your concept of God determines your miracle. This means that God's power is restricted in your life to the degree that you allow God to move. He will not force any of His children to believe in Him or love Him, just as God did not force Jesus to lay down His life. Jesus tells us in John 10:18, "No one takes it from Me, but I lay it down of Myself. I have power to lay it down, and I have power to take it again. This command I have received from My Father." This same charge we have received from our Father. The question remains, are we willing? Remember, the revelation you have of the bigness of God determines the groundwork for your belief. How big do you believe God is?

> *You can only worship and magnify God according to the picture you have of the bigness of God.*

Each person's life demonstrates what he or she believes in. If a person spends time watching television, shopping, or talking on the phone, then we know where his or her desire lies. If a person spends time serving, washing the saints' feet, taking in the poor and outcast, ministering to family and church, then we know where his or her desire lies. Their actions demonstrate to us their heart motives, desires, and focus. When we worship God in spirit and in truth, our worship will be a demonstration that God is first in our lives.

A person can only minister to God based on where God is on his or her priority list. If God is at the top of the list, then God will receive the most praise, the most love, the most ministry. However, if God is third or fourth in our daily priorities, how deep do you think our love will be for Him when we raise our hands on Sunday? So the question is, what are you spending your time worshiping? Don't misunderstand me—I did say "worshiping"! Into what do you invest your time, energy, and resources? Who and what has your attention every day? Is it God or something else? Don't tell me where you went on Sunday; tell me who you loved on Monday! Then I will know who sits on the throne of your heart, and where your devotions lie.

> *Your destiny is determined by what*
> *you praise.*

When we get up in the morning, do we praise God or do we praise food? Do we praise God, or do we praise the bathroom mirror? Do we praise God, or do we praise that snooze button? Do we praise God, or do we praise a cigarette? What is the first thing you adore when you get up? To whom and to what do you give your first moments of awake-time? God wants to be first. If you praise Him first, your destiny will ultimately be fulfilled in God's sight.

If God's bigness is not evident in your life, it is not because God does not desire to move in amazing ways, nor does it mean that He is unable to. God is just waiting for you to realize who He is and what He can accomplish if you will let Him; He wants us to worship Him according to that revelation and not according to our feelings or circumstances. To understand God's bigness is a key to worshiping God fully. For this reason, many of the prophets of the Old Covenant would retell the stories of God's deliverance in their writings. They would remind the Israelites of God's faithfulness and loyalty to His covenant. (See Psalm 78, Deuteronomy 1, Joshua 24, and 1 Samuel 10:17-19.) They were crying out to the children of Israel, "You have forgotten whom you serve! You are caught up with circumstances, instead of looking at God's reputation of faithfulness." And as the Israelites forgot what God had done for them, they also ceased to worship Him. They stopped obeying the law and followed after the pagan practices of the nations that God had conquered for them. True worship of the Lord was replaced with religion, mixture, and compromise— to the extent that idols were put up in the courts of the house of the Lord. As the house of Israel forgot God's bigness, His awesome power, and might, they lost their sense of awe and holy fear of Him and tried to make the God of the universe like some speechless idol. Holy worship ceased to exist. As believers, we must continue to meditate on God's bigness in order to worship Him in the beauty of His holiness. As your revelation of God's bigness rises, so will your worship rise.

Many people want to worship God where they are at. That is a good thing! Start where you are, but do not settle for where you are. Make sure that you allow your concept of God to grow and multiply so that your worship of God can rise to higher and higher levels of intimacy. The problem comes when we refuse to step outside our comfort zones in order to experience more of who God is. Many people are not accomplishing all they are called to do because of religion, mixture, and compromise. We have to learn to grow in the knowledge of the love of God—an intimate face-to-face encounter with the Living One. When God created man, He created Him for face-to-face, spirit-to-spirit relationships. Adam walked and talked with God in a passionate face-to-face relationship that was initiated by God. Do not assume that God wants any less with you!

> *For it pleased the Father that in Him all the fullness should dwell, and by Him to reconcile all things to Himself, by Him, whether things on earth or things in heaven, having made peace through the blood of His cross. And you, who once were alienated and enemies in your mind by wicked works, yet now He has reconciled in the body of His flesh through death, to present you holy, and blameless, and above reproach in His sight—if indeed you continue in the faith, grounded and steadfast, and are not moved away from the hope of the gospel which you heard, which was preached to every creature under heaven, of which I, Paul became a minister* (Colossians 1:19-23).

These verses carry a strong message to the reader. God has reconciled us to Himself through the blood of Jesus Christ. Because we have been reconciled to Him, He now views us as holy, blameless, and above reproach. First John 4:17 tells us that "as He is, so are we in this world." We have been restored to our places as the image bearers of God that we were originally created to be. If this is true, then there are other aspects of life in the Garden of Eden that have been restored also. For example, Jesus told His disciples, "Blessed are the pure in heart, for they shall see God" (Matt. 5:8). If we have been made pure by the blood of Jesus, then we can walk and talk with God as Adam did. There is no question in Jesus' statement—the pure in heart *will* see God! God is longing for face-to-face intimacy with His children. Our part is to reject the lies of religion, mixture, and compromise and step into the fullness of what God has for us. We were created to worship the Lord, to love Him, and to be intimate with Him. It is important to realize where God desires to take us so that we will be yielded to going there.

> Worship is a faithful human response to the revelation of God's being, character, beneficence, and will. —LaMar Boschman[8]

When you know God's character, when you are intimately acquainted with God's nature, worshiping God becomes a simple matter. When you see how big, magnificent, majestic, powerful, glorious, righteous, and loving God is, you will not be able to hold yourself back from worshiping Him! Automatically, when something miraculous happens in the world, even unsaved people cry out, "Thank God!" People who do not even call on His name give Him credit when amazing things happen. That is why the Bible tells us:

> *I have sworn by Myself; the word has gone out of My mouth in righteousness, and shall not return, that to Me every knee shall bow, every tongue shall take an oath* (Isaiah 45:23).

Therefore God has also highly exalted Him and given Him the name which is above every name, that at the name of Jesus every knee should bow, of those in heaven, and of those on earth, and of those under the earth, and that every tongue should confess that Jesus Christ is Lord, to the glory of God the Father (Philippians 2:9-11).

The Bible makes it clear that the people of the earth will see Jesus, and when they do, they *will* worship Him. Whether they know Him personally or not, whether they love Him or not, they *will* worship Him. It is the inevitable consequence of seeing God, and there is not one person who is not subject to His power. Every knee *will* bow, and every tongue *will* confess that Jesus Christ is Lord. For those of us who trust in Him the same principle applies. As we see more of God's glory, more of His power, and more of His divine influence working in our lives, the greater will be our response to Him, the more we will offer Him the worship that He deserves. When you begin to get a revelation of God's bigness, you will automatically respond, "You are My Provider! You are El Shaddai! You are Almighty!" Once you begin to meditate on all that God is and all that He does, you will respond in the same way that Jesus did when He taught His disciples how to pray: "Our Father in heaven, hallowed be Your name. Your kingdom come. Your will be done on earth as it is in heaven" (Luke 11:2). Jesus had no problem starting off His prayer with worship. If we are to follow His example, then we should worship the Lord before we begin to make our requests. We should not come before God with a long list of things we want before we have given God what He wants. Prayer should be an extension of worship. Prayer should begin with God's children pouring the oil of worship all over Jesus.

The "love of God has been poured out in our hearts by the Holy Spirit," and "God is love" (Rom. 5:5; 1 John 4:8). It is impossible to separate God from His love. As God's love is poured out in our hearts by the Holy Spirit, it is really God Himself pouring out His very being in our hearts. As we worship God, we are releasing the love of God, God's very essence and being, back to God. When we are ministering to the Lord and pouring oil on Him, we are also participating in a heavenly exchange that is rich with the symbolism of the Holy Spirit.[9]

> In worship, God is adored simply as who He is. Worship is the requital of God's love in a personal encounter, a communion which is reciprocal but asymmetrical, involving a sacrifice on the part of the created and redeemed. God calls for and enables the renewed response of worship from all believers. —LaMar Boschman[10]

God is attracted to Himself. Even though God does not need worship to survive, He enjoys it as He sees His children doing and being what He created them to do and be. Worship is reciprocal. That means that the believer offers a sacrifice to the Lord that is well pleasing and acceptable to Him as a response to the sacrifice

God already made on his or her behalf. You may ask me, "What is a well-pleasing and acceptable sacrifice to God?"

> *Worship that pleases God will always*
> *demonstrate God's nature to God.*

As we mentioned briefly before, God is not interested in anything that does not proceed from Himself. Therefore, if we are manifesting the flesh, selfish desires, or demonic influence, then God will not reciprocate. However, if we minister the activity of the Holy Spirit back to God by pouring oil on His feet, He will see His own nature and character demonstrated to Him and will reciprocate with an increase of grace—the divine influence upon the heart and its reflection in the life.

> When a small daughter crawls up on her father's lap, hugs him, and kisses him, does this make him a complete man? No. Does he have to have this? No. Does he desire and enjoy it? Oh, yes! This completes his enjoyment of fatherhood. Just so, my expressed love and adoration for God completes His enjoyment of being our Father. God loves me as an extension of Himself, and delights and receives genuine pleasure when I respond to that love in expressions of praise and worship.
> —Judson Cornwall[11]

There is only one thing in the universe that God needs: God needs God. Outside of His own being, His own omnipotence, omniscience, and omnipresence, there is nothing that God needs. That is why it is imperative that when we worship we demonstrate who and what God is so that God looks at us and recognizes Himself. Yet God desires for those who were created to be just like Him to demonstrate fully their created purpose. Paul told the church at Rome, "Will the thing formed say to him who formed it, 'Why have you made me like this?'" (Rom. 9:20). I am convinced Paul was trying to illustrate how the church and unsaved people alike want to tell God who they want to be, how they want to act, and what they want to do with their lives. God is the One who decides what you are, and it is only by loving Him that you can truly discover who God is in you. When God asks you to demonstrate His nature and character, He is asking you to be who you really are: a mirror of grace.

The word *grace* is defined as "divine influence upon the heart, and its reflection in the life, and the gratitude one should feel and express because of it."[12] Grace is what we experience as the light of God's nature and character shines down on us. God's grace is His influence, the power of His love to transform our lives so that they reflect perfectly what God is really like. Through the avenue of grace we can experience God's love as it flows through us to other people.

THE ABUNDANCE OF GOD'S LOVE

The most amazing thing about God's love is the power of

multiplication that lies within it. When we exercise our faith toward the increase of God's love in our lives, we will find that every area of our lives will be affected. The increase of God's love in our lives will lead to the increase of joy, peace, patience, and all of the fruit of the Spirit; more love leads to greater stewardship also. I truly believe that our finances will only flow to the extent that love flows from us. God will entrust us with money to the degree that He can trust us to do His will. Love has a destiny, a plan, and a vision. Love has a purpose to fulfill God's will. As God's love increases in our lives, it will become evident by how many lives we are touching, how our family life is going, and how we are distributing the blessings of the Lord.

An increase in love is a guarantor of increase in every area.

> *And this I pray, that your love may abound still more and more in knowledge and all discernment, that you may approve the things that are excellent, that you may be sincere and without offense till the day of Christ, being filled with the fruits of righteousness which are by Jesus Christ, to the glory and praise of God* (Philippians 1:9-11).

These verses demonstrate perfectly what I am talking about. We see that Paul believes that with the abundance of love comes knowledge, discernment, the ability to be accurate and excellent, sincerity, blamelessness, and the fruits of righteousness. I have heard many people pray for more discernment. I have heard people, even in my own team, say, "I need to become more accurate," or "I need to operate in a spirit of excellence." These verses make it clear that, in order to be discerning, accurate, and excellent, you must walk in an abundance of God's love. God's love is the key to spiritual growth.

Paul taught the church at Ephesus that the key to growing up into the full stature of Christ is to speak the truth in love (see Eph. 4:15). Do you see the "God working with God" connection here? Jesus is the truth, according to John 14:6, and God is love. It is possible to speak the truth without walking in love. This is when people wield the sword of the Spirit as if it were their own sword, instead of the Spirit's sword. Remember, the Spirit of God is the Spirit of love. That means when the Spirit wields the sword of God's Word He wields it for redemption, reconciliation, and restoration. The sword of the Spirit is really the weapon of love, to remove every demonic burden and destroy the yoke of the flesh.

The sword of the Spirit is the weapon of love.

I have seen and experienced firsthand what happens when a person does not speak the Word in love. You see, the Word is sharper than any two-edged sword. According to Hebrews 4:12, however, the Word is not some huge sword made to lop off arms and legs. The sword of the Spirit is a precision instrument, accurate enough to do spiritual surgery, like the tiny knives used in heart surgery. It is like a laser, with the ability to separate, even to the division of bone and marrow! Do you understand that marrow is the substance that bone is made from? And yet the Word of God can separate the two. However, when the truth is spoken outside of the context of the Spirit of love, there is no "God working with God" synergy. The truth is used like a battle axe to cut people apart; it leaves them cut the wrong way and bleeding. The Word of God, wielded by the Spirit of love, will circumcise the hearts of men; wielded in the flesh, it will make them eunuchs—unproductive and stunted.

Worship is the key to yielding to the Spirit of love. Worship builds a divine connection between the Spirit of love within us and the God of love in Heaven. Worship opens the doorway in the spiritual realm for God's love to flow like a river, from God in Heaven to God in man, and from God in man reflected back to God in Heaven. Speaking the truth in love is an amazing form of worship, because it demonstrates a yielded heart. It reveals an attitude of holy reverence for God, His Word, and His love. To speak the truth in love shows the Father that you will not use His Word according to the desires of the flesh. You will not use His Word to twist and manipulate situations. You will only use His Word as the Spirit of love directs you. Let God sharpen the weapon of love within you so that you can speak the truth in love and see God's people grow up into the stature of Christ.

GOD WORKING WITH GOD (GWWG)
LOVE AND WORSHIP

MEDITATIONS OF THE HEART

- Intimacy is the birthplace of miracles.

- Worship is releasing God's nature and character before God and toward God.

- The first Adam's choice to be fatherless was overturned by the last Adam's choice to be obedient to His Father, even unto death.

- God has called us to receive His blessing and to be a blessing to God and to others.

- Learn to worship God with your message.

- The attitude that you exude is the signature of your life.

- As we honor God for who He is and what He has done in our lives, we make room for God to work through us and in us on a daily basis.

- God honors the place of original revelation and intimacy.

- You can give without loving, but you cannot love without giving.

- Saul lost his right to be the leader over God's covenant people because he did not manifest God's covenant principles.

- You can only worship and magnify God according to the picture you have of the bigness of God.

- Your destiny is determined by what you praise.

- Worship that pleases God will always demonstrate God's nature to God.

- An increase in love is a guarantor of increase in every area.

- The sword of the Spirit is the weapon of love.

CHAPTER TWO

THE EYES OF THE BRIDE

WHAT IS WORSHIP?

Worship is the adoration, veneration, exaltation, and magnification of God. When we praise esteem, love, admire, and celebrate God, we are worshipping Him. Worship is totally concerned with the worthiness of God and not the worthiness of the worshipper. —LaMar Boschman[13]

There are many different ways to define worship. LaMar Boschman offers us a good definition to begin with. I want to discuss with you what worship is and what worship is not. Many church-going people think they are offering worship to God that is satisfactory. However, Jesus, the Son of God, put some stipulations on what we must do if we want to offer God the worship that He deserves and desires. Therefore, we must turn to God to know what the purpose of worship is and why we should do it. First let's discuss a few things that worship is not.

WHAT WORSHIP IS NOT

True worship has no motive of manipulation or flattery. To truly worship God is to carry out a completely selfless act. Worship is not self-centered; it is Christ-centered. When we walk in love, we are determining within ourselves to be Christ-centered. Praise and worship are a vital personal confrontation with God. We do not want to have need-centered song services. You cannot really call them worship services because no worship of God is going on. In fact the exact opposite is happening—people are worshiping themselves. It grieves God's heart tremendously when He sees this going on. You see, God loves to take care of His children. He knows exactly what we need and want before we ever ask Him. He delights in the prosperity of His children! God wants us to come to a place of security in Him where we do not think we must manipulate or flatter God, by singing to Him, so that we can have what we want. God is interested in our heart motive when we come to Him to worship. He knows whether we are lying in our hearts or not. He knows if we truly have come to love and adore Him, or if we are there for the purpose of merely getting our needs met. Do not misunderstand! God has already made provision for any need you will ever have. In his later years, David testified that he had never seen "the righteous forsaken, nor his descendants begging for bread" (Ps. 37:25). So, why is it, Church, that we think we should or *can* manipulate God to get our needs met? Why do we think it necessary to flatter God and lie to the Holy Spirit? God does not receive praise and worship that comes from the motive of manipulation. We must carefully examine our own hearts to ensure that we are not merely offering flattery to God so that we can be fed and warm. There is a phrase many use in the United States that perfectly demonstrates this attitude: "God bless America!" It is interesting that we see very few signs or stickers that read, "America, bless God!" Yet in the Scriptures, especially the Psalms, we see a different pattern:

Man worships God for who God is—God blesses man based on who God is.

David was a man who learned to be completely dependent on God for everything. He saw God's goodness in the worst situations: he lost family members, he experienced slander and deception; he was abandoned and mistreated by his leadership; he was made to sleep in caves and hide from enemies; his army almost turned against him; and he was forced to work for the Philistines and pretend that he was crazy. Yet in all these situations, David was more

59

than a conqueror because he knew how to depend on God. David worshiped God because of who God was, not merely to procure God's protection. And as David worshiped the Lord, God made a way through every difficult circumstance.

> *Bless the Lord, O my soul; and all that is within me, bless His holy name! Bless the Lord, O my soul, and forget not all His benefits: who forgives all your iniquities, who heals all your diseases, who redeems your life from destruction, who crowns you with lovingkindness and tender mercies, who satisfies your mouth with good things, so that your youth is renewed like the eagle's* (Psalm 103:1-5).

You see in the above verses that David was continually reminding his soul—his mind, will, and emotions—that God was faithful. Because of who God is, David instructed his soul, "Bless the Lord!" David recognized that, even though he could rely on God for everything, he should not merely worship God because he found himself in a bind. God was worthy of worship no matter what was happening in the natural! In another psalm, David says, "His praise shall continually be in my mouth!" (Psalm 34:1). When we love God, we should realize that God wants to be appreciated for who He is, not merely for what He can give us.

In summary, we have discussed that:

Worship is not manipulation or flattery; worship is also not self- or need-centered; worship should not be used as a means of procuring provision or getting what we want.

When we approach God, we should remember that God desires to be loved for who He is, not merely for what He can give us.

THE PURPOSE OF WORSHIP

Let's take a closer look now at what the purpose of worship is and why God's children are called to do it. Most believers have a desire on a regular basis to worship the Lord in different ways. It is as if they were made to do it. You will hear them say, "Praise the Lord!" when something good happens, or "Thank God!" when a person escapes harm or lives are saved. People who love the Lord can be heard singing at work, at home, and in the car! Why is that? Yes, there is a reason other than that they are out of their minds! The truth is all humans were created to worship.

YOU WERE CREATED TO WORSHIP

Within every human being is the pattern of God. In those who are unsaved this pattern has not been activated. Their true self lies dead, waiting to be resurrected by the power of Jesus Christ. When a person accepts Jesus as Lord and is filled with the Holy Spirit, this person's real self, which thinks, looks, acts, and talks just like Jesus Christ, is made to live. Supernatural salvation restores a person to their original created self: an image bearer of God. God created man in His image and likeness, to be and do all that God is and does. So then the question is, what is God? As First John 4:17 tells us, "as He is, so are we in this world"; this same chapter explains to us clearly what He is and, therefore, what we were created to be:

> *Beloved, let us love one another, for love is of God; and everyone who loves is born of God and knows God. He who does not love does not know God, for God is love. In this the love of God was manifested toward us, that God has sent His only begotten Son into the world, that we might live through Him. In this is love, not that we loved God, but that He loved us and sent His Son to be the propitiation for our sins. Beloved, if God so loved us, we also ought to love one another. No one has seen God at any time. If we love one another, God abides in us, and His love has been perfected in us. By this we know that we abide in Him, and He in us, because He has given us of His Spirit....Love has been perfected among us in this: that we may have boldness in the day of judgment; because as He is, so are we in this world. There is no*

fear in love; but perfect love casts out fear, because fear involves torment. But he who fears has not been made perfect in love. We love Him because He first loved us (1 John 4:7-13,17-19).

God is love! Love is the very essence of God's nature. Love is not merely an aspect of who God is; love is not just one of His many characteristics. God and God's love are one and the same. Every other aspect of God's nature and character proceed out of love. Holiness, righteousness, mercy, faithfulness, kindness, gentleness, justice, excellence, and so many other attributes of God are the overflow of love. If this is how the nature and character of God functions, then this is the supernatural pattern that has been placed within our spirits to which we are to be conformed. Let's look closely at what the Scripture tells us concerning what God has created us to be. Below are just a few verses, all found within the Pauline epistles, that tell us that man was created to be the image bearer of God. Remember to go back and look at the context of each verse in your personal Bible to catch the full meaning of what Paul is conveying.

For whom He foreknew, He also predestined to be conformed to the image of His Son, that He might be the firstborn among many brethren (Romans 8:29).

As was the man of dust, so also are those who are made of dust; and as is the heavenly Man, so also are those who are heavenly. And as we have borne the image of the man of dust, we shall also bear the image of the heavenly Man (1 Corinthians 15:48-49).

But we all, with unveiled face, beholding as in a mirror the glory of the Lord, are being transformed into the same image from glory to glory, just as by the Spirit of the Lord (2 Corinthians 3:18).

Do not lie to one another, since you have put off the old man with his deeds, and have put on the new man who is renewed in knowledge according to the image of Him who created him (Colossians 3:9-10).

God has called us to be His image bearers. He has called us to be conformed to the image of the Son. God is love, and in order to think like God, speak like God, and act like God, we must walk in love. Therefore, our number one love relationship must be with God. The only way we will learn to love like God is to be loved by God and to love Him in return. As the apostle John mentions in the above verses, we can only love God because He has already loved us and made a way for us to have intimate relationship with Him. In the intimate place with God, we will learn to receive God's love, to love God back, and to love others with the love of God. The mysteries of God's Word are revealed to those who are in deep intimacy with God. Moses, who wrote the first five books of the Old Covenant, called the Torah, spent a total of 80 days on the mountain experiencing face-to-face encounters with God (see Exod. 24:18; 34:28). Although we do not know exactly what happened between God and Moses, we do know that God allowed Moses to see His back, the trail of His glory (see Exod. 33:23). We also know that Moses heard God's audible voice speak to Him. We know that in this place of deep intimacy God's law was spoken and received. We see this same pattern in the life of Jesus and Paul: Jesus fasted for 40 days; He experienced, received, and manifested God's glory; He was the voice of God in the earth; He was the Word of God become flesh. Paul, the apostle to the Gentiles, went to the desert for a period of time (see Gal. 1:17); he did not confer with flesh or blood, but sought God's face. According to Second Corinthians 12:2, Paul was caught up in the spirit into the third heaven and saw Paradise. He heard unutterable words while He was there and experienced God's glory. From this experience Paul wrote two-thirds of the New Testament. The revelation of God's Word came from a deep place of intimacy with God.

This same place of intimacy is what God has created for all people to experience with Him. Intimacy with God is not just for apostles and leaders. God has designed every person to have a close, intimate relationship with Him. If we desire for God to reveal to us the deep things of God, we must draw close to Him in worship. Every relationship takes an investment of time, energy, and resources. Our relationship with God is no different. We must realize that the deepness of our intimacy with God will determine exactly how far we can go in intimacy with other people. Our relationship with God is the most important relationship that we will ever have and must be made the number one priority in our life. When we refuse to put God first in our life, we are denying the very reason why we were created: to worship the Lord. We are created for love—love first from and for God. A firm love relationship with God enables us to develop loving relationships with others out of that foundation of security and grace.

Being the Bride

What does it mean to be a bride? It means to be totally enraptured with the love of the bridegroom. It means to encourage and yield to the intimacy that the husband desires. It means to exalt, venerate, admire, encourage, respect, defer to, and uphold the bridegroom. To be the bride means to be the lover of the bridegroom. It is only when we are loving Jesus with all of our being that we can truly minister God's love to the nations. Works that are born out of love are the only works that count at all! The rest, First Corinthians 3:12-13 tells us, will be burned up like hay, chaff, and stubble. So, as a corporate Body let's not forget what we were created to do: we were created to worship God, we were created to be the Bride of Christ, and we were created to love others as God loves them.

You see, God has instilled within us the desire to worship. He has designed us to be intimately acquainted with the truth. This God-given desire has been twisted and distorted in many people because they have never come face to face with the knowledge of God. Unsaved humans will still continue to worship even if they do not know God. They worship things, possessions, money, comfort, each other. They know that they were created to worship, and so they do it with their whole hearts: they worship nicotine; they worship alcohol; they worship sports. They worship their children; they worship the good old days; they worship food. They worship their jobs; they worship their lifestyle; they worship the Internet. They worship their right to be free, their right to be safe, and their right to be educated. Most of all, humans worship themselves. Yet, with all their trying they still hunger for more and will never be satiated outside of intimacy with God. Since the Garden of Eden, God has been calling people to worship Him.

What Is God Looking For?

Worship is the avenue by which we return to the place of intimacy.

As we stated earlier, the first act of intimacy recorded in the Bible took place between God and Himself. God came face to face with God. The Spirit of God went to work with the Word of God, and "the Word of God became flesh" (John 1:14); all of creation was birthed from this act of intimacy. We see this pattern take place in another place in the Bible: it happened when a simple young woman believed the Word of God and received it. When Mary, the mother of Jesus, told the angel, "Let it be to me according to your word" (Luke 1:38), she was really saying, "I believe it, and I receive it! Let your Word come to pass in my life!" When she spoke and received God's Word, she became the incubator for the Word of God. As the angel said, the Holy Spirit then came and hovered over that Word. Just as the Spirit of God had come face to face with the Word of God in the first chapter of the Bible, so God's Spirit and God's Word were coming face to face as the Spirit hovered over Mary. Once again, "the Word of God became flesh and dwelt among us" (John 1:14). The act of intimacy between God and Himself once again created a perfect work: Jesus Christ.

Jesus told us that God's Words are spirit and life (see John 6:63). When Mary received the Word of God, she was receiving what was of the spirit. Any time we receive what is of the spirit, we are giving God something to work with, because God will only work with what is of God. Do you remember what Jesus told the woman at the well?

> God is Spirit, and those who worship Him must wor-
> ship in spirit and truth (John 4:24).

God is looking for something when He watches our worship. We see in James 4:5 that the "Spirit who dwells in us yearns jealously." He is not yearning for beautiful music if that music does not come from the depths of His Spirit. God is jealously desiring Himself! God is looking for the Spirit of God and the Word of

God when He looks at us. He is looking for the manifestation of the Word of God becoming flesh. God is looking for a face-to-face contact between God in Heaven and God in you! Worship will take you to the place where God's Spirit within you and God in Heaven are face to face. And in this place of deep intimacy, miracles are birthed.

Let's look at the story of creation again. This time I want you to look at chapter 2, verse 7. A key to understanding our purpose in worship is seeing how God has enabled us to do just that. It is important that we understand that all true worship ushers forth from God.

> *And the Lord God formed man out of the dust of the ground, and breathed into his nostrils the breath of life; and man became a living being* (Genesis 2:7).

God breathed into Adam the breath of life. The truth is that God came face to face with Adam. God was intimate with His creation, with the man who was made to be just like God in every aspect. It is important to note that God did not come face to face with every animal, nor did God make every part of creation to be His image bearer. Only the man was made in the image and likeness of God. The implication of this truth is that man was the only created being who could be intimate as God was intimate: face to face. Man was the only created being who could love God back with the same passion and intimacy that God had within

Himself. Man was created to reflect perfectly God's deepness of intimacy.

Verse 7 tells us that the act of God's breath entering Adam's body took him from dust to a living soul. Adam was first a physical being; however, when God breathed into him, he became a spiritual being. The Hebrew word used in this verse that we translate as *soul* is actually the word *nephish*.[14] This word means to take in breath; however, according to Dr. Wheeler, this word carries an even stronger connotation:

> It means to literally draw breath from the Spirit of God, total dependence upon God for everything, even the very breath that one takes. *Nephish* contains no idea of either mortality or morality. It is total innocence. There is no idea of corruption, death, or decay in this word and certainly no idea of sin.[15]

Dr. Wheeler indicates that the life, the very thing that God instills within us, is wrapped within the very nature of God's purity, holiness, and innocence. God's intention with His children is that worship will return them to a place of complete holiness, consecration, and innocence before Him. God's eyes "run to and fro throughout the whole earth," looking for those whose "heart is loyal to Him": the heart described here will be in passionate pursuit of God—pure, holy, and innocent (see 2 Chron. 16:9).

*God is passionately pursuing a heart
like God's.*

Salvation is the process of trading in a heart that is full of iniquity for a heart that has an innocence like the soul—*nephish*—had in its original state. The heart of iniquity is called *lev* in Hebrew, and the word is used to describe the heart or center of man's being after the Fall. This heart is subject to death and corruption; it is not innocent because it is not fully dependent on God for everything. The heart of iniquity tries desperately to be independent, self-sustaining, and self-fulfilling. The heart of iniquity is manipulative and full of flattery. It is self- and need-centered. *Lev* causes us to view every relationship as a means to gain what we need and want. Salvation is the process of turning over this *lev* in exchange for *nephish*. You see God is completely innocent. His Spirit is the spirit of holiness and innocence. That is why the Bible teaches us that if we desire to be righteous before God we must be clothed with the robes of righteousness by God Himself. Self-willed efforts to be what God desires will never please God; only a heart that is dependent on God can truly please God.

HOW CAN TWO WALK TOGETHER?

Every human relationship created by God was meant to mirror God's relationship to Himself. The first human relationship was meant, first, to mirror the relationship that God had with Himself, and, second, to mirror the relationship that God had with Adam. Eve was created to mirror Adam in every way. When God put Adam to sleep, He took a piece of Adam to use as the building blocks for the woman. She had his exact DNA! She was made to complement Adam in the way that Adam complemented God. The man was made to receive from God. The woman was made to receive from man. The man was made to be God's companion. The woman was made to be man's companion. The man was enabled by God's love. The woman would be enabled by God's love in man. In a very similar fashion, the woman is to give to her children as the man has given to her. She takes what she learns from the man and imparts it to her small ones. That is why the man had to be a perfect image of what Father God was. If the man was not, the woman would not receive the correct picture of God.

Do you see that without the woman, man could not have been fully like God? For God is a giver. God is a lover. God is the Father. God is a protector. In order for man to manifest fully the nature and character of God, Adam needed to have someone to give to, someone to love, someone to lead, someone to protect. In this way the woman completed the man. As he gave life to her, so she brings this life back to him, and in this way she completes the image of God![16]

Each relationship was created to mirror God. However, we must keep our eyes open and see how the devil twists what God has created to mirror His nature in order to create idolatry. The woman was not created to take the place of the Father. When she ate of the fruit of the tree and offered it to her husband, she was laying a choice before him: you can either do what seems good in my eyes, or you can do what is good in the Father's eyes. Eve was no longer completing man at this point, because she was not infusing him with the life of God which she was created to give him. The man rejected his Father for another father: satan. Because the woman was deceived, she was used as a doorway by the enemy to bring death to the man. Adam's sin lay in the fact that he rejected his Father. Adam had allowed Eve to rise to the level of the kiss of God on his life, and this is idolatry.

God created woman to complete man; she was a perfect match for him, spirit, soul, and body. She breathed life from the same Spirit that Adam breathed life from. In Second Corinthians 6:14, we are told not to be "unequally yoked." Remember, the yoke was a long piece of wood with two cord loops hanging from it. The yoke was used to bind two oxen or horses or cattle together so that they could pull something heavy behind them. The yoke was used to combine the strength of the two animals. If the owner put one animal that was healthy and strong and one that was small, weak, and sickly in the yoke, the larger animal would have to do all the work, which would eventually destroy its strength. When God created Eve, He made her strong in the spirit, so that she would be a good partner for Adam. God did not make her weak and sickly so that Adam would have to do all the work. This would have gone against God's very nature, for when God created Adam to be His teammate, He created him just like God. He created him to be a perfect image of who God is. Adam was created to be nothing less than all that God is. In the same manner, Eve was created to be nothing less than all that Adam was. She was "bone of his bone and flesh of his flesh." Therefore, as they worked together, Eve would have been a perfect match for Adam. She was not exactly the same as Adam, as the man was not exactly the same as God. God remained the Creator, and man remained the creature. Yet, Adam was created to reflect perfectly who God is so that God would be able to yoke Himself with a man.

You see, God will not be unequally yoked together with unbelievers. God will not be in relationship with anyone but God. You may tell me, "Warren, that disagrees with Scripture. Jesus said, 'Take My yoke upon you.' God wants us to be in the yoke with Jesus" (see Matt. 11:29-30). That is very true. However, we must not forget that God has called us to be conformed to the image of the Son. He wants Jesus to be yoked with people who think, talk, act, and look just like Jesus!

God is looking for agreement. He loves to find his children in unity. He loves to see His children behaving as a body would—each part fulfilling its function as part of the whole. He despises factions among the Body—a toe over there doing its own thing, unconnected to the head; the stomach having fits because of unholy emotions; the brain thinking thoughts of rejection and abandonment; the feet walking in different directions. When this is the case, we are like the body of the nations of Judah and Israel seen by the prophet Isaiah:

Alas, a sinful nation, a people laden with iniquity, a brood of evildoers, children who are corrupters! They have forsaken the Lord, they have provoked to anger the Holy One of Israel, they have turned away backward. Why should you be stricken again? You will revolt more and more. The whole head is sick, and the whole heart faints. From the sole of the foot even to the head, there is no soundness in it, but wounds and bruises and putrefying sores; they have not been closed or bound up, or soothed with ointment (Isaiah 1:4-6).

When we come to worship God, what are we demonstrating before God? During the week, are we gossiping and slandering people in the Body we don't like or agree with? Are we walking in judgment and criticism against God's delegated authority in the church? When we go to our workplace in the world, are we doing our work as unto the Lord, or are we lazy, apathetic, and carnal, just like those workers who do not know Jesus? If these things are the case in our hearts, and we stand before God to raise our hands and voices in praise, I promise you, brothers and sisters, God will not hear us. God wants spiritual agreement. That means we must bring our lives into agreement with God's Word, which is spirit and life. God wants to be intimate with a pure and spotless Bride, a Bride that thinks, talks, acts, and looks just like Him. And God has grace and mercy to purify His Bride and strengthen the intimacy of the Church. He will settle for nothing less than all that He is; we can trust that as we yield to Him, God will transform us into exactly what He wants us to be. Jesus wants us to take on His image so that we can be equally yoked together to fulfill God's purposes.

Remember that the Scripture teaches us that in the last days, the watchmen of God will see eye to eye (see Isa. 52:8 NKJV, Darby). That means their words will be in agreement with God and with each other. They will no longer fight and bite at each other, using the prophetic mantle as a covering for bitterness, gossip, and strife. God detests this. People who operate in this way may sing songs about God, but God does not hear them, for God can only hear God. We do not want to be like the Pharisees, of whom Jesus cried, "Well did Isaiah prophesy of you hypocrites, as it is written: 'This people honors Me with their lips, but their heart is far from Me. And in vain they worship Me, teaching as doctrines the commandments of men'" (Mark 7:6-7). When we worship God from the Spirit of God, we will be offering God what He desires. This attracts God to us; it will also help us to grow in even greater intimacy with God.

SPIRITUAL PERCEPTION

A powerful key to worship is the sharpened perception of the spirit. To have the sharpened perception of the spirit is to be able to see what God sees in us, in other people, and in specific situations. Jesus told the Pharisees, "I speak what I have seen with My Father..." (John 8:38). Jesus made the claim that He could actually see what God was saying. There have been many times when I have been in revival meetings in which the Holy Spirit is moving in a powerful way to bring prophetic words to people in the congregation. It is easy to tell who among the people have been meditating on God's Word. As I speak the word of wisdom or word of knowledge over them, those who believe God's Word will begin to glow, and their eyes will light up. Their spirit says to me, "Yes! I believe what God says! I can see where God is taking me!"

A practical example of this comes from the stories of David. From the time he was a young lad, David had been anointed king; and though he had the symbol of authority poured out on his head, it took many years before David was made king. Saul was a man of great stature, taller than anyone else in the land. He was good looking and came from a good family. (See 1 Samuel 9:1-2.) The people of Israel liked him because they had no vision. They were blinded by Saul's good looks instead of seeing what was in his heart and where his heart would take them in the future. The people were shallow, manipulative, and easily manipulated. Above all they were deceived. Because they could not see God's bigness, His faithfulness, and His steadfast covenant love and devotion, they rejected God from being their King. They proclaimed, "Now make us a king to judge us like all the nations" (1 Sam. 8:5). They could not see where a human king would take them because they had forgotten God's law. Deuteronomy speaks expressly about the issue of a human king. The book was a prophetic message from Moses, in which he warns the Israelites *not* to seek out a human king to rule over them. Moses promised them that a human king would bring them into bondage and dictate his own will over the land instead of God's (see Deut. 17:14-15). Moses had vision. He knew the hearts of the people and warned them beforehand of what was coming. Because the children of Israel had forgotten God's law, they lost their ability to see.

Because Saul rejected the word of the Lord, God rejected Him and chose another to be king: a man after God's own heart. God told Samuel, "Do not look at his appearance or at his physical stature....the Lord looks at the heart" (1 Sam. 16:7). It is interesting to note that the first tribe to recognize David as king was the tribe of Judah (see 2 Sam. 2:4). The name *Judah* means "praise" in the Hebrew language. "Praise" was able to recognize God's delegated authority, whereas the rest of the tribes remained fragmented for several years. You see, praise and worship open our spiritual eyes to see what God is saying concerning God's true chosen leadership.

Many people in the church cannot recognize true apostolic authority when it enters the church building because they do not spend much time looking at the Lord! The more time a congregation spends in the secret place having intimacy with God, the easier it will be to recognize and submit to God's delegated human authority. Why is that? It is because when we look at the person God has chosen, we will see what God says about that person. We will see God and not a mere man. We will see God's Word taking on flesh right before our eyes. We do not want to be like the Pharisees who could not recognize who Jesus was. Because their hearts were far from God, their worship tainted and shallow, they could not look at the Son and see the Father. All they saw was a mere mortal, and how wrong they were. In the same way, we tend to judge and criticize God's leaders in the church because we are not seeing what God says about them. We make our own opinions and reject the word of the Lord. When we do this, we are being like the people of Israel and like the Pharisees.

Remember God reveals His secrets to those who are intimate with Him. If we are being intimate with God, hearing His deep and intimate thoughts, it will be easy for us to recognize God's counsel coming out of another person's mouth.

The ability to hear the difference between the pure Word of God and mixture rests in intimacy.

It is very important that we stay in the place of worship all the time so that we will be able to hear God's voice clearly and have vision for the future. In my own conscience I make a decision to choose to reverence and respect what is of God in me and those around me. When I stay in the state of constant reverence and respect to God in me and in others, I have assurance that the leadings of God can be absolutely trusted when my footsteps are taken in the love of God. Therefore, the confidence of God's leading voice is concrete in me because I know that the voice of God proceeds out of the love of God.

Our time spent in worship can be the deciding factor for whether or not we fulfill the highest call of God on our lives. If worship opens our eyes to see clearly what God has for us, then it is imperative that we remain in God's presence. God may send specific people into your life in order to stir you up or to bring correction to you. He may send a spiritual father or mother to you to train you for a higher calling. However, if you are not being intimate with God it can be easy to miss those divine relationships. Even now, there is probably a specific person or persons who come into your mind when I speak of authority. Remember, God sees God. If you are looking at your spiritual leadership and you can't see God, then it is most likely a problem with your perception, not with their character. God put that person in your life for a reason—to sharpen you and mentor you. However, you will never truly receive your full inheritance until you see in that person what God sees![17] Worship will sharpen your spiritual perception so that you can see what God is saying.[18]

COME WITH ME, BELOVED

But also for this very reason, giving all diligence, add to your faith virtue, to virtue knowledge, to knowledge self-control, to self-control perseverance, to perseverance godliness, to godliness brotherly kindness, and to brotherly kindness love (2 Peter 1:5-7).

When I read this verse, I am convinced that each character trait listed is really another level of intimacy with God. Scripture makes it clear that each person is given a measure of faith (see Rom. 12:3). Faith is foundational in our love relationship with God. Hebrews 11:6 tells us that "without faith it is impossible to please Him, for he who comes to God must believe that He is...." In the Greek, the word *pistis*[19] (we translate this word as *faith*) and its derivatives are used twice, once for the word *faith* and once for the word *believe*. To have faith is to believe, to be fully persuaded that God is a big God. Faith says, "I can jump because my Daddy will catch me." Without this quality of faith, it is impossible to draw near to God at all. Many people might then say, "I have faith. That is enough." Yet the apostle Peter makes it clear in the above passage that God intends for faith to be a building block, a cornerstone in the beautiful structure He has created you to be. Peter tells us, "add to your faith virtue..." The word *virtue* means moral excellence. When I consider what it means to be morally excellent, I see a picture of a faithful and devoted wife who fully comprehends the desires and instructions of her husband, and does them with a willing and obedient heart. God is a jealous God and is deserving of our whole devotion; He should not have to share the throne of our hearts with other gods. We are in a courtship of love with Jesus Christ. Hosea chapter 2 makes it clear that we are to have one Husband; if the Lord has to share us with other lovers, I promise you, He will not be happy!

The next level of intimacy spoken of in Second Peter chapter 1, is the level of knowledge. Even under the Old Covenant, the knowledge of the Lord was something that was a key to being a friend of God. The words *to know* in the both the Hebrew and the Greek carry the connotation of intimate acquaintanceship and communication. The words were used to describe all aspects of marital intimacy, including sexual intimacy, under both the New[20] and Old Covenants.[21] We can see then that to add knowledge to virtue would be to move from a courtship of love to the place of face-to-face intimacy. When we look at the verse through this light, it takes on a whole new meaning. God wants us to grow in our intimate walk with Him from the place of courtship to the place of marital intimacy with Him.

THE COMMANDMENT OF LOVE

When Jesus was asked what the greatest commandment of the law was, He replied, "You shall love the Lord your God with all your heart, with all your soul, and with all your mind" (Matt. 22:37). We are commanded to love God, not when we feel like it, and not when it's convenient for us! God does not want partial devotion or partial obedience. He wants your whole being. God wants your heart: He wants to sit on the throne of your heart. He wants to rule in your inner man, your spirit, the very essence of who you are. God wants your soul: God wants your emotions, feelings, and desires to be toward Him and for Him. God wants your mind: God wants you to be devoted to Him in your decision realm. He wants to know that every day you will choose to love Him, and that you will set your mind like flint to worship Him. We are commanded by God to love Him; yet we must *choose* to be obedient to the commandment of love. Like any relationship, there are times when the "feeling" wears thin. There are times when difficulties arise that must be dealt with. When these situations occur in a marriage, we must choose to love our wife or husband. We must choose to continue in delight and devotion to them. Within our intimate relationship with God, it is the same. Each day we must choose to go to the secret place and be intimate with God. He is ready all the time! The Lord is waiting for us to respond to His pursuit.

LOVE THE LORD WITH YOUR EMOTIONS

God wants our souls to be trained to love God by walking in holiness. It is easy to worship God with your emotions when everything seems to be going your way. I believe that God receives more worship, however, when we walk in peace and holiness when it is difficult to do so. When we allow unholy emotions to rule us, we are not worshiping God with our emotions. When we are touchy, unkind, and easily offended toward the people around us, we are not worshiping God with our soul. In this way we are being an unfaithful wife to our gentle, loving Husband. At times it may feel as if your soul is chafing against the yoke of Jesus Christ. Your emotions may want to put on another yoke, or just to be free without any commitments at all. Yet if we allow our emotions to rule us, we will be taking on the worst bondage of all: that of the flesh. Instead of being intimate with the Lover of our souls, we will be committing a carnal act with the dead man! Remember Jesus prepared Himself for a pure, spotless, and holy Bride, a Bride without wrinkle, a Bride without defect (see Eph. 5:26-28). In order to be this kind of Bride, we must love the Lord with all of our soul as well as our spirit. The Bible teaches that God's *agape* love is not self-seeking, rude, self-indulgent, puffed up, easily offended, or touchy. God's love never fails, and God's love has been poured out in our hearts by the Holy Spirit. (See 1 Corinthians 13:4-8 and Romans 5:5.) We must allow God's love to rule over our emotions and feelings. When our mind, will, and emotions line up with the love of God, we will be offering the kind of worship to God that He can receive and deserves: worship birthed out of His own love.

God only works with a motive that is driven by love.

It is so important that we yield our spirit, soul, and body to the love of God. Covenant love keeps us in a place of abiding in God so that God can continually work with Himself. That is what marriage is: it is an eternal covenant, sealed by the shedding of blood. When we manifest God's steadfast covenant love and devotion through acts of worship, we are really saying, "Jesus, You are my Husband. I am devoted to You. You are my Champion. I believe in You." When our spirit, soul, and body line up with our words, Jesus is truly glorified as our Husband. We are then being the crown and glory of our

Lord. And, truly, the face-to-face experience will only come when we have sanctified ourselves, spirit, soul, and body. For God can only come into unity with God. We are called to be one spirit with the Lord (see 1 Cor. 6:17). This is a great mystery, yet it is the truth of God's Word. If our desire is to be one with God, we must allow our emotions to come into alignment with God's purposes. Genuine worship will never hinder the purposes of the Anointed One and His anointing. Genuine worship comes out of pure love. When we express pure love to God through genuine worship, we will begin to tap into the deep things of God's Spirit as He takes us from one level of intimacy to the next.

> ..."Eye has not seen, nor ear heard, nor have entered into the heart of man the things which God has prepared for those who love Him." But God has revealed them to us through His Spirit. For the Spirit searches all things, yes, the deep things of God. For what man knows the things of a man except the spirit of the man which is in him? Even so no one knows the things of God except the Spirit of God (1 Corinthians 2:9-11).

It is only in the deep place of the Spirit of God that the deep things of God will be revealed. The Spirit of God knows the deep things of God and will reveal them to us if we will just draw near to worship Him with a pure heart. God's secrets are for those who are walking in the intimate, covenant relationship prepared for those who will receive it. Let me demonstrate what I mean: You see, any time you see the word *love*, you can replace it with *God*. Any time you see the word *God*, you can replace it with *love*. So let's try it in this verse: "Eye has not seen, nor ear heard, nor have entered into the heart of man the things which God has prepared for those who [God] Him." When we love God with His steadfast covenant love, we are really "God-ing" Him: exalting the Godhead, giving Him the preeminence, making Him and His nature and character the Ruler of our lives and everything around us. When we love God we are releasing God's nature back to Him.

In the next verse let's replace the word *God* with the word *love*: "For the Spirit searches all the things, yes, the deep things of [love]. For what man knows the things of a man except the spirit of man which is in him? Even so no one knows the things of [love] except the Spirit of [love]." In this context we really get a picture of how dependent we are on God in order to release His love correctly. Only love can reveal love! When we worship the Father, we are really allowing the Spirit of love to adore, magnify, exalt, and honor love. We are utterly reliant on God for access to the deep things of His love. As the Bride of Christ, it should be our goal always to allow the Spirit of love to adore the God of love in Heaven.

The Spirit of love adores, magnifies, exalts,
and esteems the God of love.

Love the Lord by Listening

I have noticed something that is very powerful about my wife. She always takes the time to look me in the eye and listen to what I have to say. I am convinced that she thinks the words I speak are valuable because of the way she treats me when I am speaking. Whether we realize it or not, it is a simple thing to tell a person's intimacy level with God by the way they behave during a sermon. A Bride who is enraptured with the voice of her Beloved will come excited to hear the Word of the Lord. She will take notes and teach the things she learned to other people. She is excited about what her Husband is doing and what He has planned.

Jesus has given us a good example in this area. Many times Jesus would spend all night in prayer, listening to God (see Luke 6:12). Jesus was extremely devoted to the voice of God! He told the Pharisees, "Whatever I speak, just as the Father has told Me, so I speak" (John 12:50). As His Bride, the Church should strive to make this statement our goal. Listening and taking notes in church is an excellent way to show God that you value, esteem, respect, and desire His Word. We should realize that what the man of God is sharing with us, he heard while he was in the secret place with the Father. When we disrespect our leadership, we are really disrespecting our Husband, Jesus Christ.

As we begin to listen to God's Word, it will be the Spirit within us responding to that Word who will produce God's nature and character in us. The Spirit of God will rise up to work with the

Word of God. As we value, respect, honor, esteem, and desire God's Word in our lives, God's Word will be multiplied back to us in revelation, the gifts of the Spirit, and the fruit of the Spirit. God's Spirit will work with God's Word. This is the "God working with God" principle. The church is getting fat on all the revelation that is coming forth through mighty men and women of God, yet we still see a decline in church growth, fewer souls saved, and less unity in the Body! Beloved brethren, this should not be so! Jesus taught us that to whom much is given, much will be required (see Luke 12:48). Our Great Husband has given us bountifully from His Word. Now we must take it and multiply it by bringing souls into the Kingdom. God has called us to sow God's Word into others so that God can work with His Word to produce a harvest of God.

THE DECEPTION OF TRADITION

God has called us to have a spirit-to-spirit relationship with Him. God in Heaven desires to be face to face with God in us. We are called to know Him as we are known and to walk and talk with Him. We are called to reflect His glory and emanate His nature and character. We are called by God to worship Him, to exalt Him, to honor Him, to love and adore Him. We are called to be yoked together with Jesus Christ, a perfect match for the King of kings. Yet there is something that stands in the way of the Church as a whole. And yes, it is a BIG something! It is a huge wall that has been built for centuries with the goal of separating us from true intimacy with Christ. This wall is called tradition.

Let me explain: Paul told the Thessalonians they were to hold fast to the traditions given them by the word spoken to them, or by the letters written to them (see 2 Thess. 2:15). Within this verse we see two very important aspects of God's Word: namely, the *articulate utterance, both written and spoken (logos)* and the written letters from Paul (*epistole*). Paul is telling them that any tradition that accepts and practices both the spoken and the written Word is to be honored and adhered to. The problem comes when one of the two are ignored. You see, *rhema* is birthed out of *logos. Rhema is* the revelatory expression of the written Word of God. *Rhema* gives voice to the command of God on a personal application. It brings to life a verse or passage that the Spirit of God has touched and brought greater revelation or insight through. Without the written Word of God, there would be no *rhema*—as there would be no Jesus (the Word become flesh) without the Father (the One who spoke the Word). Yet, in order for the *logos* to take on voice in a person's life, it must become *rhema* to them. It must be touched by the Spirit of God, so that it can become personal revelation that transforms a person's heart. The point is, if you have *rhema* without *logos*, you get flakey prophetic people whose words are full of mixture. The *logos* of God, the written Word of God, which carries the voice of God, takes on a greater strength in people's lives when the Spirit of God is allowed to work with the Word of God.

A great example of this happened between Saul, the first king of Israel, and Samuel the prophet. Samuel was sent by God to inform Saul that he was to destroy the Amalekite people. Saul was to kill every living thing, all the people and their livestock. Nothing was to remain alive (see 1 Sam. 15). This story will be discussed in even greater depth in a later chapter; right now I want you to see one very important principle: the prophet of God came to Saul and spoke the *rhema* word. This rhema word was based in the written Word, the *logos*: namely in Exodus chapter 17, verse 14. Because of a great offense against Israel many years earlier, God had promised to utterly destroy Amalek. Now God was sending Saul to accomplish His *logos* Word (see Exod. 17:14) through the mouth of the prophet who spoke God's *rhema* word. Samuel was speaking according to the Spirit of God and the Word of God. The Spirit of God was working with the Word of God to bring to pass God's will.

However, a problem occurred. Instead of doing exactly what Samuel had instructed Him to do, Saul decided to do things apart from the *rhema* word of God. Saul brought back the best of the livestock to offer as sacrifices to the God of Israel. He also brought back Agag, king of the Amalekites to kill in front of the army. According to the *logos*, this behavior was not incorrect. God had ordained the sacrifice of animals to Himself, and had even allowed Moses to kill the kings whom he conquered (see Num. 21). Saul walked in the footsteps of his fathers, following the traditions of the peoples who went before him. And yet what he did was unrighteous, for he chose tradition over obedience; he followed the commands of the written

Word of God and ignored the spoken word of the prophet, sent to him by God.

Under the law, to sacrifice animals to the Lord was an acceptable form of worship. If a man sacrificed, he was showing God that he loved the Lord and was obedient to His Word. It may have appeared that Saul was having intimacy with God, worshiping Him as he was commanded to do. This is the deception of tradition. Tradition gives the appearance of intimacy. Tradition knows how to keep the law, fulfill the ordinance, and walk the line. Tradition knows all the right things to say and all the formulas to use. Even so, it is the farthest thing from intimacy. As Jesus told the Pharisees:

> *Woe to you, scribes and Pharisees, hypocrites! For you pay tithe of mint and anise and cummin, and have neglected the weightier matters of the law: justice and mercy and faith. These you ought to have done, without leaving the others undone. Blind guides, who strain out a gnat and swallow a camel! Woe to you, scribes and Pharisees, hypocrites! For you cleanse the outside of the cup and dish, but inside they are full of extortion and self-indulgence. Blind Pharisee, first cleanse the inside of the cup and dish, that the outside of them may be clean also. Woe to you, scribes and Pharisees, hypocrites! For you are like whitewashed tombs which indeed appear beautiful outwardly, but inside are full of dead men's bones and all uncleanness. Even so you also outwardly*

appear righteous to men, but inside you are full of
hypocrisy and lawlessness (Matthew 23:23-28).

Do you see what Jesus is saying to the Pharisees? These men were the religious leaders of the day, the heads of the Jewish community. They even gave tithes and offerings! Can you imagine if your pastor got in the pulpit next week and called up the five largest givers in his congregation, just to tell them, in front of a crowd of people no less, that they needed to repent for hypocrisy? I highly doubt that it would happen! Yet God was not impressed by the financial giving of the Pharisees. Why, do you ask? He was not impressed because they were not really fulfilling His Word by what they were doing. They were putting on a show of love and intimacy with God, while in their hearts they had rejected Him. Many people are interested in putting on a good show for other church members. They come to church looking sharp, dressed well, with all their children in a row. They raise their hands and sing loudly. Yet, when they get home, they scream at their spouses and kids. Their houses are in shambles, and the things of the flesh are given an open doorway through their television sets, radios, and computers. They say, "Praise the Lord!" on Sunday, but on Monday they worship carnality, rage, gluttony, and many other things. These people are not being intimate with God. They are playing a game and fooling only themselves.

This game is the game of the unfaithful wife. She says, "Oh, I love you," when her husband is at home, but slanders him to her friends when he is away. She says, "I am devoted to you," but flirts with other men at work. She is a cheat, a manipulator, and a liar; and in the end she will only end up destroying herself. Jesus is looking for a Bride who will be yoked with Him, reflecting back to Him His perfect image of holiness, faithfulness, and love. This is the church He will bless, honor, esteem, and cause to grow. This is the worship He will accept because it is birthed out of the nature and character of God. Remember, Matthew 15:8-9 tells us that God could see right through those hypocritical Pharisees. He told them, "These people draw near to Me with their mouth, and honor Me with their lips, but their heart is far from Me, and in vain they worship Me, teaching as doctrines the commandments of men." God is not fooled by tradition. God is looking for what is of God.

Tradition is moved more by mechanics and dynamics than by the Spirit of God.

Remember that unless the Lord builds the house, those who labor, labor in vain. Mark 7:7-23 takes it even further. Within these verses there are seven principles that separate true worship from tradition.

1. Verse 7: Tradition teaches as doctrines the commandments of men.
2. Verse 8: Tradition lays aside the commandment of God.

THE DIVINE ATTRACTION

3. Verses 10-12: Tradition does not show proper respect for elders and leaders.

4. Verse 13: Tradition makes the Word of God of no effect.

5. Verse 15: The traditions of men proceed out of inner defilement.

6. Verse 15: Tradition magnifies the outside appearance while ignoring inward corruption.

7. Verses 21-23: The heart of tradition is full of every kind of evil.

Jesus made it clear that it is what lies within a man's heart that will determine what comes out of a man's mouth. These are the things that will either condemn him or acquit him. If God proceeds out of a man's mouth, God will be attracted to what is of His nature and character, and acquit that man. By his words, every man will be judged because out of the abundance of the heart the mouth speaks (see Luke 6:45). You see, God is listening to our mouths. He wants to know what is enthroned on our hearts. When we bless God from a pure heart, we are offering true worship to the King. However, we must watch that we do not become like the Pharisees and the unfaithful wife. Putting on a show for ourselves and for others will not impress God because God is only impressed by God.

> In this you greatly rejoice, though now for a little while,
> if need be, you have been grieved by various trials, that

the genuineness of your faith, being much more precious than gold that perishes, though it is tested by fire, may be found to praise, honor, and glory at the revelation of Jesus Christ (1 Peter 1:6-7).

Genuine faith will always be tested by fire. The Scriptures teach us that God sits as a refiner of gold. God puts us in the fire to find out what is in us: when dross comes to the surface, He does not pretend it is something of value. He scrapes it off and throws it in the fire. If we allow God to work His will in our lives, the dross will continue to come to the surface until we are the purest gold, a gold without spot or blemish. This is God's intention: to produce after His own kind by destroying any deception, tradition, compromise, and mixture that stands between us and His image. God will purge out and burn up anything that hinders God from working with Himself within us.

Jesus perceived the wickedness of the Pharisees' hearts. At times Jesus would perform miracles in a certain way in order to make manifest what was on the inside of them. In Luke 14:5, Jesus told them clearly that they cared more about donkeys and oxen then they did about the children of God! He was pointing out how ludicrous their traditions were, which placed animals above men. The Pharisees were always angry with Jesus for healing on the Sabbath. He healed a paralyzed man and a crippled woman on the Sabbath. In one instance, Jesus merely commanded the man to stretch out his hand, and without touching him, healed the man (see Matt. 12:13). It is obvious that the Pharisees and religious leaders of

Jesus' day could not recognize God's authority within Jesus. Yet, we know that had they truly been worshiping God, loving and honoring Him, they would have recognized the One they loved within His Son. In this way, it is obvious that they were not truly worshiping God, because the God of love has the ability to recognize the God of love within others.

> **The God of love within you has the ability to recognize the God of love within others.**

Worship takes us into a place where we can receive a greater perception of who God is, His glory, His nature, His power, and His majesty. We gain a greater knowledge of God as we press into the intimate place with Him. There are certain levels of revelation that God only releases access to through intimacy. There are times when we want God to merely "download" His knowledge and wisdom from Heaven to us without much effort on our part. Yet we need to remind ourselves that it is the glory of God to conceal a matter, and the glory of kings to search it out (see Prov. 25:2). God may conceal something from us for a time to see if we will pursue Him. Remember the picture drawn for us in the book of Song of Solomon:

> *By night on my bed I sought the one I love; I sought him, but I did not find him. "I will rise now," I said, "And go about the city; in the streets and in the squares I will seek the one I love." I sought him, but I*

did not find him. The watchmen who go about the city found me; I said, "Have you seen the one I love?" Scarcely had I passed by them, when I found the one I love. I held him and would not let him go, until I had brought him to the house of my mother, and into the chamber of her who conceived me (Song of Solomon 3:1-4).

Throughout the book of Song of Solomon, we see that the Beloved is constantly searching for his love. He comes and calls to her through her window. He comes to her by night. Yet it is interesting that in this passage, it is the lover, the woman, who is seeking her Beloved, with the expectation that she will find him. She is driven by her love for him and will continue to search until she can hold him in her arms again. In this passage, I really believe that the watchmen symbolize a place of deep prayer, a spirit-to-spirit contact with God. When we enter into deep prayer seeking God with all our heart, mind, soul, and strength, intimacy is inevitable. Thus the woman says, "Scarcely had I passed by [the place of intercession] when I found the one I love." Prayer took her to a place where she could see her Beloved face to face. This is a call to the Bride of Christ to do the same: to seek the Lord, to press in to know Him, to seek Him through deep intercession, and to not give up until you have had a face-to-face encounter with the Bridegroom.

Listen, brothers and sisters, when Jesus spoke before the multitudes He spoke in parables, shrouding His words so that they would remain blind and deaf. Yet when He spoke to His disciples, Jesus revealed the deeper meaning to His words. He uncovered the revelation to those who were close to Him, those who loved Him, and those who followed Him. He revealed secrets to them of His death, burial, and resurrection, which He never told the multitude. Jesus imparted to them of His very being, even telling them when His soul was greatly sorrowed in the Garden of Gethsemane. Those who were intimately acquainted with Jesus were the ones commissioned by Jesus to go into all the world and preach the Gospel. It was these people that He commanded, "Heal the sick, cleanse the lepers, raise the dead, cast out demons" (Matt. 10:8). When we are intimate with the Lord, He will reveal to us the hidden secrets of His heart, as a husband does with His wife when they are alone. A man does not blurt out his feelings around everyone. He holds them in and may pretend that nothing is wrong with him. However, when he is alone with his wife, he reveals the way he truly feels. God longs for this kind of intimacy with us. He wants us to freely receive what He has laid up for us.

Church, today we are the Bride of Christ. God has called us, not to be conformed to this world, but to be transformed by the renewing of our minds, that we may prove what is that good, and acceptable and perfect will of God (see Rom. 12:2). God desires a Church that is a living sacrifice, holy and acceptable. God wants our hearts and minds to be turned toward Him at all times, offering to Him the worship that He deserves as the King of the entire universe. We must realize that Jesus is not interested in a dead, apathetic, gossiping, lazy, manipulating, busybody of a wife! Jesus will not be unequally yoked. He wants a Bride who is spotless, pure, holy, and washed in the water of the Word (see Eph. 5:25-27). Jesus gave us the example, as God did for Adam and Eve in the garden: live your life as a sacrifice. Take up your cross daily and follow Me (see Luke 9:23). Humble yourself, even unto death. Because as far as this world is concerned, you have died, and your real life is hidden with Christ in God! (See Colossians 3:3.) Worship is sacrifice. And God is looking at your heart to find out what it really cost you.

To Capture the Heart of the King

During the days of Queen Esther, there were both written and unwritten laws that controlled the behavior within the court of the king. One of these laws was that no one was to come before the king without having been summoned. Not everyone had access to the king whenever they felt like it. This was to bring control and order to the kingdom. If everyone was always coming before the king, all of the needs of the people would fragment the king's focus and destroy his ability to see the big picture. Yet, we know that Esther was able to approach the king without being summoned. She broke the protocol of the kingdom and dishonored the written and unwritten laws of the king.

For some reason, however, she was able to do so and live. The reason is that she had captured the heart of the king. The king had chosen her above all other women in the kingdom to be his queen; she was called out and priceless to him. As the Bride of Christ, we must make it our desire to capture the heart of the King of kings. In the Song of Solomon, the Bridegroom tells the Bride, "You have ravished my heart, my sister, my spouse; you have ravished my heart with one look of your eyes, with one link of your necklace" (4:9). What a powerful hold the Bride had on her Bridegroom's heart. He was completely ravished by her, and all she had to do was look at him. I am convinced that when he looked into her eyes, he saw a reflection of his own love there and was attracted to that reflection. This is the kind of love God wants to have between us and Him. There is only one person who can truly ravish the heart of the King of kings, and that is a Bride who perfectly reflects who He is back to Him.

When we approach the King of kings, He wants to see us shining with the radiance of His holiness, clothed in spotless garments. Jesus does not want us to come before Him covered in guilt, shame, and condemnation. The Lord cannot accept these things. That is why He continually washes His Bride with the water of the Word: so that He, Jesus, can present us, the Bride, to Himself, Jesus. Jesus, the Son of God, is the One who does what is necessary to the Bride in order to produce what is of God in us so that He can present the Bride to Himself. For only God can produce God. Allow God within you to make you into a spotless Bride, perfect in holiness and righteousness, in order to present you to Himself. Allow the worship of God from within the Spirit of God to rise within you to meet God in Heaven, and touch the face of God. This is when true intimacy will occur, and God's nature and character will be birthed.

GWWG LOVE AND WORSHIP

MEDITATIONS OF THE HEART

- Man worships God for who He is—God blesses man based on who God is.

- Worship is not:
    Manipulation
    Flattery
    Self- or need-centered
    A means to procure provision
    A means of getting what we want.

- You were created to worship.

- You were created to love God.

- You were created to be the Bride of Christ.

- You were created to love others as God loves them.

- You were created to be blessed and to be a blessing.

- Worship is the avenue by which we return to the place of intimacy.

- God is passionately pursuing a heart like God's.

- The ability to hear the difference between the pure Word of God and mixture rests in intimacy.

- God only works with a motive that is driven by love.

- The Spirit of love adores, magnifies, exalts, and esteems the God of love.

- Tradition is moved more by mechanics and dynamics than by the Spirit of God.

- The God of love within you has the ability to recognize the God of love within others.

CHAPTER THREE

WORSHIP IS CREATED IN THE HEART

WHERE YOUR TREASURE IS

Do not lay up for yourselves treasures on earth, where moth and rust destroy and where thieves break in and steal; but lay up for yourselves treasures in heaven, where neither moth nor rust destroys and where thieves do not break in and steal. For where your treasure is, there will your heart be also (Matthew 6:19-21).

Jesus taught us that it is a simple thing to tell where a person's heart lies: the thing that a person gives time, energy, and resources to is the thing he or she worships. For some it could be their jobs; for others, it could be their families. For even still others, it might be something seemingly darker, such as alcohol or drugs; it could be pornography or other forms of perversity. To worship is to bless, exalt, adore, and reverence. Worship is a sacrificial act of giving part or the whole of one's self to another person or thing. Everything we do in life is an act of worship to something. When we go to the grocery store, who are we worshiping? God, gluttony, fear, an eating disorder? If we so choose, our every action can be a sacrifice of worship to God.

Loving God is an issue of the heart. When people asked Jesus what the greatest commandment was, He replied, "You shall love the Lord your God with all your heart..." (Mark 12:30). According to Hebrew thought, the heart was the seat of emotional responses *and* of knowledge and wisdom.[22] In Mark 12, Jesus quoted a verse from Deuteronomy 6:5. It is important to look closely at the word choice used by the Hebrew writer (Moses) in this verse. The word *chosen*, which we translate as *love*, is the Hebrew word *ahab*, which is "basically... equivalent to the English 'to love' in the sense of having a strong emotional attachment to and desire either to possess or to be in the presence of the object."[23] This word for love is very important because it signifies three distinct areas of love: sexual intimacy, covenant friendship, and total loyalty between slave and master. Each manifestation of love proceeds out of the heart.

When we examine the Hebrew word for love, we will actually see our own relationship with God reflected as we grow in our understanding of Him and our love for Him. When new Christians are first saved, they only have a small amount of knowledge concerning God. They know that God saved them; they know that they belong to God; and they respond to God's goodness purely because of what He gives them. This can be compared to the relationship of a slave to his master. At this level of relationship there is no true intimacy. Yet as we grow in our knowledge of God—who He is and not just what He gives us—we will begin to love Him more. Our relationship with God grows into a friendship. We begin to trust Him and admire Him for His own nature and character. We are still just as needy and reliant on Him as before, yet He is more than just our Provider. Now He is our Friend. Again the more we know God the more we grow to love Him. As this love deepens into grave honor and respect, our relationship with God should develop into an intimate face-to-face encounter with God, the kind of love that a man and wife share. This is what God desires to have with us. However, many Christians never make it past the first stage of *ahab*. They are bound in the slave/master relationship because of lack of knowledge. As I stated earlier, the heart is both the center of emotional responses and wisdom and knowledge. Without the knowledge of God, it is impossible to love Him. Our emotional response will flow from encounters with God, as we learn who He is and what He has done for us. Your heart is the throne of your life, and the knowledge you have is what decides who and what sits on that throne. Who and what do you know? With whom and what are you intimately acquainted? Is it the Lord God or another, lesser, counterfeit?

Then God blessed them, and God said to them, "Be fruitful and multiply; fill the earth and subdue it; have dominion over the fish of the sea, over the birds of the air, and over every living thing that moves on the earth." And God said, "See, I have given you every herb that yields seed which is on the face of all the earth, and every tree whose fruit yields seed; to you it shall be for food. Also, to every beast of the earth, to every bird of the air, and to everything that creeps on the earth, in which there is life, I have given every green herb for food"; and it was so. Then God saw everything that He had made, and indeed it was very good. So the evening and the morning were the sixth day (Genesis 1:28-31).

Genesis chapter 1 teaches us that when Adam and Eve were first created, God spoke blessing over them. The first words which Adam and Eve heard God speak were blessing. The Scripture teaches us that out of the abundance of the heart the mouth speaks (see Luke 6:45).

But what does it say? "The word is near you, in your mouth and in your heart" (that is, the word of faith which we preach): that if you confess with your mouth the Lord Jesus and believe in your heart that God has raised Him from the dead, you will be saved.

For with the heart one believes unto righteousness, and with the mouth confession is made unto salvation (Romans 10:8-10).

First we must believe in our hearts. Jesus must come to sit on the throne of our hearts through experiential knowledge of Him before confession can be made unto salvation. In other words,

---

In order for God to come out of a man's mouth in confession, that man's heart must first be ignited with belief.

Adam and Eve had received the spoken blessing of God; they had received experiential knowledge of God's blessing, which, we stated earlier, is a key part of worship. This experience set them up to enter into God's atmosphere of worship by speaking blessing over God and over each other. Adam and Eve were only able to bless God to the degree that they had received God's blessing in their hearts. Remember that God created an atmosphere of worship in the Garden of Eden that was perfect; the love that Adam and Eve shared with God was not tainted by sin. They were without sin; they had received the blessing of God perfectly and they manifested reverence and honor to God in a perfect manner. A perfect manner means that Adam and Eve's worshiping of God came from a pure heart without fear, wrath, or doubting. It was the reflection of God's own love flowing through the image of Himself that He created. First Corinthians chapters 12 and 13 tell us that love is the more excellent way. The more excellent way ruled and reigned in the relationship that God had with Adam and Eve.

God's love pervaded all of their existence until the enemy came and sowed seeds of deception. The seeds of deception questioned God's love—has God really said? Can you believe God? Can you trust God? Are you really like God? Remember that doubt and unbelief are sin. When a person steps into the realm of doubt and unbelief, they are stepping out of the realm of faith. Hebrews 11:6 tells us that without faith it is impossible to please God. Fear, doubt, and unbelief are contrary to faith. When you step into doubt and unbelief, you are believing the report of the enemy instead of what God says. You are acknowledging the principles and lies of the enemy as your master. You are claiming that the enemy has greater power in your life than God. Christians need to understand the power of recognizing God's Lordship over their lives. When the thief hung on the cross next to Jesus, he said, "Lord, remember me when You come into Your kingdom" (Luke 23:42). Whenever a person recognizes the Lordship of Jesus, Jesus is going to possess what is His. Immediately He said to the thief, "Today you will be with Me in Paradise!" The thief experienced salvation because he identified Jesus as his Lord.

The Scripture teaches us that we are to love the Lord our God with all our heart. We know from First John 4:8 that God is love. Let's reword this verse to say, we shall God the Lord our God with all our hearts. When we reword the verse this way, we are once again recognizing God's position in our lives. We are crowning Him King by saying You are God; You are love. Love is now ruling and reigning in my life. Romans 8:28 says:

> *And we know that all things work together for good to those who love God, to those who are the called according to His purpose.*

Again, we can rephrase this verse to say, "all things work together for good to those who God God." All things work out for those who release God's own nature and character back to Him; all things work together for good to those who recognize God's Lordship over their lives. Paul told us in Romans 5:5 that the love of God has been poured out in our hearts by the Holy Spirit. In order for God's love to be released through us back to God in worship, God's love must be poured out in our hearts. God's nature and character can only be demonstrated through us to the degree that we have assimilated that behavior in our own lives. This is the principle of reflection. A mirror can and will only reflect what it captures in front of it. A mirror cannot reflect the face of a person who is not looking into it. The Scripture teaches us that we are God's mirror; God desires to look into us and see His own perfect love mirrored back to Him; yet, unless He looks into the mirror, we will never be able to reflect back who He is (see 2 Cor. 3:18). The mirror is just a copy of the original; it can be an excellent copy, without blemish, yet it is still a copy. We are called to be copies of the master Copy, Jesus Christ. We are called to be mirrors of God's grace and love.

You can only worship God to the degree that you allow love that has been shed abroad in your heart by the Holy Spirit to flow.

Jesus told His disciples in Matthew 5:8 that the pure in heart will see God. What does this mean? It means that only those who have God's purity can recognize God, for only God recognizes God. It is impossible to look upon God with impure, unholy eyes. Paul tells us in Titus 1:15, "To the pure all things are pure, but to those who are defiled and unbelieving nothing is pure; but even their mind and conscience are defiled." A defiled mind cannot comprehend the holiness of God. Only that which is holy can receive God's holiness. The same principle pertains to God's love. We can only love God to the degree that His love dwells and rules in our hearts.

A CHOSEN PEOPLE

Blessed be the God and Father of our Lord Jesus Christ, who has blessed us with every spiritual blessing in the heavenly places in Christ, just as He chose us in Him before the foundation of the world, that we should be holy and without blame before Him in love (Ephesians 1:3-4).

These verses paint a clear picture of the "God working with God" relationship that brings us into a place where we can worship God. Paul tells us that God has blessed us with every spiritual blessing in Christ [God] and has chosen us in Him [God] before the foundation of the world that we should be holy [God's character] and without blame [God's nature] before Him [God] in love [God].

God chose you to be face to face with God in God.

The Greek word translated *before* in verse 4 is the word *katenopion,* which "signifies 'right over against, opposite', always in reference to God. 'Before' (God as judge), 'in the sight of' (God), 'in His sight,' before the presence of (His glory)."[24] This draws a powerful picture of our position in God—face to face with Him. He chose us in Him to be in this position before time began.

> *But you are a chosen generation, a royal priesthood, a holy nation, His own special people, that you may proclaim the praises of Him who called you out of darkness into His marvelous light* (1 Peter 2:9).

God chose you before the foundation of the world to be one of His own special people. God set you apart for a specific purpose. The power of redemption is in the fact that it brings humans back into a place of righteousness where they can properly praise God.

Only what is set apart by God can praise God.

The only worship that God will accept is His own perfection. This may seem like a hard saying. Yet, we have to recognize that all we have to give God is what we have received from God in the first place.

> *Cause me to hear Your lovingkindness in the morning, for in You do I trust; cause me to know the way in which I should walk, for I lift up my soul to You (Psalm 143:8).*

> *Behold, You desire truth in the inward parts, and in the hidden part You make me to know wisdom. Purge me with hyssop, and I shall be clean; wash me, and I shall be whiter than snow. Make me hear joy and gladness, that the bones You have broken may rejoice (Psalm 51:6-8).*

Jesus told us in John 14:6, "I am the way, the truth, and the life. No one comes to the Father except through Me." This is confirmed by the above verse that tells us that God desires truth in the inward parts. God desires to see what is of His nature and character in our inward parts. This will attract God to what is of the truth, what is of His nature and character within us.

Make me understand the way of Your precepts; so shall I meditate on Your wonderful works....Make me walk in the path of Your commandments, for I delight in it. Incline my heart to Your testimonies, and not to covetousness (Psalm 119:27,35-36).

He has put a new song in my mouth—praise to our God; many will see it and fear, and will trust in the Lord (Psalm 40:3).

O Lord, open my lips, and my mouth shall show forth Your praise (Psalm 51:15).

Let my mouth be filled with Your praise and with Your glory all the day. ...My mouth shall tell of Your righteousness and Your salvation all the day, for I do not know their limits. I will go in the strength of the Lord God; I will make mention of Your righteousness, of Yours only. O God, You have taught me from my youth; and to this day I declare Your wondrous works (Psalm 71:8,15-17).

In these verses, the psalmist demonstrates his utter dependence on God for the ability to open his mouth and praise the Lord. Worship is both from God and toward God; that is the reason why unsaved people cannot offer true worship unto God. God knows the difference between worship that is birthed out of His own nature and character and mere "lip service." Remember, God is only impressed by Himself. God is only attracted to Himself. In order for God to respond to our worship, He must find something of His own heart within our praise.

> *He answered and said to them, "Well did Isaiah prophesy of you hypocrites, as it is written: 'This people honors Me with their lips, but their heart is far from Me. And in vain they worship Me, teaching as doctrines the commandments of men'"* (Mark 7:6-7).

Jesus is pointing out that though words that sounded like worship—perhaps even Scripture verses like the ones above—were coming out of these men's mouths, their hearts were not worshiping God. This was their number one problem. A man's words may line up with the Word, but we must be able to discern whether or not God sits on the throne of his heart. Second Chronicles 16:9 tells us that the eyes of God are going to and fro over the face of the earth looking for a heart that is loyal to Him. This is an interesting choice of words in the Hebrew, because the word translated *loyal heart* is actually the attribute "perfect." The Hebrew word here is *shalem*, which comes from the root *shalam*. Both words mean *complete, whole, perfected*, and most often are applied to God and His Word.[25] Basically this verse is telling us that God is searching for a heart that manifests the nature of God. He is looking for Himself, and when He finds

Himself, He shows Himself strong on behalf of Himself. God is not impressed by anything that does not remind Him of Himself.

God is looking for a loyal heart, a heart like His. I appreciate the use of the word *loya,* because of the strong picture loyalty paints concerning how God expects us to behave toward Him. The word translated *loyal* in the New King James Version of the Bible is translated as *perfect* in the King James Version, and is the word *shalem.* If we say that a loyal heart is one that perfectly mirrors God's purposes and will, this takes the word *loyalty* to a whole new level. The word *shalem* in Hebrew demonstrates a different aspect than the word for faithfulness, which is *aman. Aman* describes the love of a parent to a child, steadfast, firm; concerning the faith of a believer, *aman* means to trust God.[26] So, we see that to be faithful to God is to trust Him; to be loyal to God is to perfectly mirror His will. Faithfulness is to love God; loyalty is to hear His voice. Faithfulness is to know God's Word; loyalty is to allow the instructions of God to become concrete in you through practical application. In the realm of faithfulness, there can still be disunity; in the realm of loyalty, there is complete unity of vision. In the realm of faithfulness, a person can still question. In the realm of loyalty, the clarity of God's voice silences doubt.

FACE TO FACE

A lukewarm heart cannot perform boiling hot worship, nor can a rebellious life revere God with any depth of sincerity. —LaMar Boschman[27]

When I visit churches all over the world, I can always tell how the church is growing spiritually—not by the number of members or the size of their choir, but by watching their worship. Are they really pressing into God? Is their hunger for God's manifest presence obvious in their body language and words? Do they sing to God with all of their being? Or do they hold back? Do they sit uninvolved while others worship? Are they excited, or are they apathetic?

When we look closely at the original language that the New Testament was written in, we can receive a clear understanding as to the level of intimacy we were created to have with God in worship. The Greek word most frequently translated as *worship* in the New Testament is a combination of two distinct Greek words: *pros* ("toward, face to face")[28] and *kuneo* ("to kiss").[29] This word is vividly intimate and can even be interpreted in a playful and candid manner. It should be obvious that God is expecting a demonstration of passion and excitement. He is not impressed by an uninvolved, uncaring attitude. To praise God is not a shallow action.

> **Worship is the natural outflow of a consecrated heart.**

Worship extends out of the attitudes and feelings of the heart. The Bible speaks of numerous expressions of worship: clapping the hands, kneeling down, spinning around violently, dancing, shouting, etc. All of these acts of worship flow out of what is enthroned in a person's heart. It is a true statement that our emotional responses flow out of what is enthroned in our hearts. If we have a revelation that God is huge, then our emotions will manifest His bigness. If we have revelation that God is YHWH Shalom, the Prince of Peace, we will manifest the peace of God in our emotions. Worship is merely the outward expression of what lies in our hearts toward God. If we are bound by religion, the bondage will manifest when we come to worship. If we are listening to fear or condemnation, these things will manifest in our emotions in worship.

> ### The genesis of worship is in the heart of a believer.

Remember, an unbeliever cannot truly worship God because we worship to the degree that God's love has been shed abroad in our hearts. Without the love of God already at work within us, it is impossible to manifest God's love toward God. Worship is recognizing God's bigness—that He is magnificent. Heart attitudes are the key ingredients of worship. Do we take God lightly? We know that Jesus told the disciples, "Be careful what you are hearing. The measure [of thought and study] you give [to the truth you hear] will be the measure [of virtue and knowledge] that comes back to you—and more [besides] will be given to you who hear" (Mark 4:24 AMP). This applies in the area of worship as well. If we value who God is and what He is doing in our lives, it should be natural for us to praise and worship Him.

Worship requires holiness. The four living creatures around the throne of God cry, "Holy, holy, holy, Lord God Almighty, who was and is and is to come!" (Rev. 4:8). Christians need to realize that they do not cry out "love, love, love" or "mercy, mercy, mercy"; there is a reason which binds them to proclaim God's holiness. Not just anyone can approach the living God. Remember what God said to Moses: "Take your sandals off your feet, for the place where you stand is holy ground" (Exod. 3:5). When the high priest approached God in the Holy of holies once a year, his body had to be clean, and his clothes washed and purified by the sprinkling of the blood. He could not be ceremonially unclean or defiled; if he was and dared approach God, the high priest would fall down dead. Our God is a holy and living God who expects us to approach Him out of holiness. He told His people,

> For I am the Lord your God. You must consecrate yourselves and be holy, because I am holy. So do not defile yourselves with any of these small animals that scurry along the ground (Leviticus 11:44 NLT).

> Give the following instructions to the entire community of Israel. You must be holy because I, the Lord your God, am holy (Leviticus 19:2 NLT).

> They [the priests] must be set apart as holy to their God and must never bring shame on the name of

God. They must be holy, for they are the ones who present the special gifts to the Lord, gifts of food for their God (Leviticus 21:6 NLT).

The camp must be holy, for the Lord your God moves around in your camp to protect you and to defeat your enemies. He must not see any shameful thing among you, or He will turn away from you (Deuteronomy 23:14 NLT).

For I have chosen this Temple and set it apart to be holy—a place where My name will be honored forever. I will always watch over it, for it is dear to My heart (2 Chronicles 7:16 NLT).

And I gave them My Sabbath days of rest as a sign between them and Me. It was to remind them that I am the Lord, who had set them apart to be holy (Ezekiel 20:12 NLT).

Just as He chose us in Him before the foundation of the world, that we should be holy and without blame before Him in love (Ephesians 1:4 NKJV).

God's will is for you to be holy, so stay away from all sexual sin (1 Thessalonians 4:3 NLT).

So you must live as God's obedient children. Don't slip back into your old ways of living to satisfy your own desires. You didn't know any better then. But now you must be holy in everything you do, just as God who chose you is holy. For the Scriptures say, "You must be holy because I am holy" (1 Peter 1:14-16 NLT).

I am sure that these verses make it clear to you that it is God's will for us to approach Him in holiness. There is a pervading philosophy in the church that it is impossible to be holy. It is a lie. Second Peter 1:3 tells us, "As His divine power has given to us all things that pertain to life and godliness, through the knowledge of Him who called us by glory and virtue." Yes, His divine power has given us all things that are necessary to live holy lives before God. He even predestined that we would be holy (see Rom. 8:28-30). Holiness is a prerequisite for worship and a product of entering into covenant with God. God chose us to be a holy generation; we were born not of the will of the flesh, nor of the will of men, but of God. We have God's genetic make-up. This means we have the same ability to be holy that God has.

I will betroth you to Me forever; Yes, I will betroth you to Me in righteousness and justice, in lovingkindness and mercy (Hosea 2:19).

Husbands, love your wives, just as Christ also loved the church and gave Himself for her, that He might sanctify and cleanse her with the washing of water by the word, that He might present her to Himself a glorious church, not having spot or wrinkle or any such thing, but that she should be holy and without blemish (Ephesians 5:25-27).

God does not want us to approach Him in ungodliness and unrighteousness. He wants a pure and spotless Bride, washed in the water of His Word. As a revivalist traveling from church to church, I have seen the product of unfaithfulness within human relationships; it is very hard to trust a person who is unfaithful, and many husbands and wives divorce because of one act of infidelity. Sometimes, however, we do not see that in our actions we are being unfaithful to God. We put evil before our eyes in the form of secular media and worse, and then on Sundays, we want to enter into God's presence and be intimate with Him. God, however, looks at us as a man looks at an unfaithful wife. When we sin and choose to love the things of the world instead of God, we are cheating on the King of Heaven. This is unholiness, which has to be dealt with before we can truly enter into the intimate place with God. The blood of Jesus is what makes us clean, and if we meditate on the Word of God, His promises will keep us in the place of holiness.

ENTER HIS GATES

The Scripture makes a differentiation between praise and

worship; however, in their specific applications or physical demonstrations, they may overlap each other. Praise is repeating back to God all the wonderful works He has done throughout time and in your life. Praise is much more horizontal, meaning that praise is used to encourage the people around us to enter into praise also. Praise is what draws everyone in the congregation in and gets each person involved in the service. This is what Psalm 100:4 means when it says, "Enter into His gates with thanksgiving, and into His courts with praise." Praise is made to get everyone's attention. It is as if the leader is saying, "Hey everyone, let's go up to the house of God together!"

Praise is when we begin to exalt God for His mighty acts and great deeds. Many people never move past this stage. There is one important aspect to praise that we must discuss: praise is a form of warfare. When we praise we have the power to break barriers that hinder us from entering into the intimate secret place with God. We will discuss the power of praise in warfare in more detail in Chapter Six. Many bondages of fear and condemnation can be broken in praise. The truth is, without praise it would be impossible to enter into real worship of God. Worship without praise is like intimacy without communication. As a husband I realize if I do not speak loving and kind words to my wife periodically throughout the day, she may not be willing to yield in intimacy at the end of the day. Why is that? I have not built any kind of bond with her through my words. The same is true with God. Praise is like the red carpet for God's presence. God's power will always bloom in the aftermath of praise.

WHAT MAKES GREAT WORSHIP?

Many times, worship leaders get caught up with the trimmings of worship: arrangement, instruments, tempo, etc. Yet these things mean nothing if God is not the center of our activities. I have been in revival services where one young man with his guitar was more powerful than a whole worship team; his focus on God was like a laser beam that split the heavens and brought down the glory. He was less concerned with how he sounded than on whom his desire was set.

A God-focused heart is a laser beam that splits the heavens and brings down the glory.

One a cappella singer with a heart that is passionate about the Father will usher in the glory of God more quickly than pretty songs and a large choir that has no real love for God. Our hearts are the issue; Proverbs 4:23 says, "Keep your heart with all diligence, for out of it spring the issues of life." What is coming forth from your heart is going to determine the direction your life will take. If unbelief, fear, worry, and doubt are coming forth from your heart, then you are going to head in that direction; however, if the love of God is coming forth from your heart because God the Father is enthroned there, then God's will and purposes are going to rule in your life. You will head in the direction of your words; your meditation determines your destination. So, if you want to become a worshiper of God, you must set the inner thoughts of your heart on God and on His bigness.

Smith Wigglesworth, a mighty evangelist from England at the turn of the last century, spent three hours in worship every morning and raised many people from the dead. This is something to consider. He set his mind on God from the moment he rose from his bed. Remember, what you do in private determines your level of accomplishment in public. We have to have a revival in our private lives before we can have one in corporate worship.

If you can't win the battle in private, you won't win the battle in public.

What you do in private shows what your heart issue is. It is a simple thing to hide our attitudes from other church members; if your pastor could observe your quiet time unseen, what would he learn about you then? It is a serious question. Many worship leaders, elders, deacons, churchgoers, and even pastors spend little to no time in the presence of God. This is not only affecting their own love relationship with God, but it is also affecting the growth of the whole Body. Whether you are a leader in the Body of Christ or not, your private life affects everyone around you. You are part of a Body, and if even the smallest toe or the elbow hurts, the whole Body cannot flow to its fullest potential. Ask yourself, how is my personal time with Jesus helping to move my church family forward in the things of God? Am I a hindrance or a help? Am I a buoy or a barnacle?

.

And by this we know that we are of the truth, and
shall assure our hearts before Him (1 John 3:19).

John chapter 1 tells us that when the Word of God became flesh, "we beheld His glory, the glory as of the only begotten of the Father, full of grace and truth" (John 1:14). We know that when God's Word becomes flesh we will behold His glory full of grace and truth. Remember, John 4:24 tells us that those who worship God must worship Him in spirit and in truth. The reason that we do not see God's Word becoming flesh in our lives is because we are not hiding God's Word—His truth—in our hearts. There is only one way according to the Scriptures that we can assure our hearts before God—that is, to walk in the truth by hiding God's Word in our hearts. If we choose to hide God's Word in our hearts, then the truth, Jesus Christ, the Word become flesh, will be enthroned in our hearts; what is enthroned in our hearts determines the direction our worship takes. This is why Jesus warned so strongly against lustful thoughts. When a man looks at a woman and lusts after her in his heart, he has immediately dethroned God's Word in his heart and enthroned lust and deception. Trust has been replaced with lust. The lustful image first penetrates your thoughts, and then it works its way into your heart. This is the plan of the enemy: to replace thoughts of trust with thoughts of lust, so that his images will sit on the throne of your heart instead of God's truth. In order to guard against this problem, Jesus taught that we should guard our eyes. Matthew 6:22-23 says:

*The lamp of the body is the eye. If therefore your eye
is good, your whole body will be full of light. But if
your eye is bad, your whole body will be full of darkness. If therefore the light that is in you is darkness,
how great is that darkness!*

We must guard our eyes, because our eyes are like a window
into our hearts. Whatever we put before our eyes is going to end up
in our hearts. What we look upon with our eyes determines the state
of our whole body. We have to be like Job who said, "I made a
covenant with my eyes, how then should I look lustfully at a young
woman?" (Job 31:1 WEB). We must make a covenant with our eyes
that we will only look upon those things that are holy, pure, righteous, noble, honorable, virtuous, and lovely.

*For if our heart condemns us, God is greater than our
heart, and knows all things. Beloved, if our heart
does not condemn us, we have confidence toward
God* (1 John 3:20-21).

I do not want my heart to condemn me. I want to have assurance and confidence toward God. I want to be able to come with
boldness into the throne room to receive grace and help in the
time of need. When a person struggles with condemnation, it is
very difficult for them to come into God's presence. They continue to hold back from truly worshiping God because their

hearts tell them they are unworthy to worship Him. What these people do not realize is that condemnation is just another name for pride. When we refuse to receive the forgiveness and grace of God because of condemnation, we are claiming that we know what we deserve and God does not; this is pride. Christians need to realize that Jesus spread out His hands on the cross for them; He spread out His hands to conquer sin, hell, death, and the grave for them! With this knowledge, how can we remain unwilling to spread out our hands to tell Jesus that we love Him? How much do you love God? How much do you appreciate what Jesus has done for you?

Many times people who cannot worship God with freedom do not truly understand what it cost Jesus to die for them. It cost Him everything! Listen friend, loving you cost Jesus everything He had—His throne, His heavenly position, His dignity, His comfort, His health, His life! Jesus laid down everything He had when He took on the form of a servant and became obedient unto death. That is why God has highly exalted Him. If the Father, the God of Heaven has highly exalted His Son, we must join in exalting Him, for it was for our lives that He laid down His all. It grieves the Holy Spirit when a person who has partaken of God's goodness will not express their gratefulness and love back to God in worship.

Why do we assure our hearts before God? Because allowing our hearts to be assured before God is a form of worship. Assuring our hearts before God deals with the problem of misdirected worship.

Because, although they knew God, they did not glorify Him as God, nor were thankful, but became futile in their thoughts, and their foolish hearts were darkened (Romans 1:21).

We can see from this verse that thankfulness is a key to strong worship. Our hearts must have a spirit of gratitude. Gratitude being amplified out of the heart is a powerful force to break barriers that hinder us from moving into a greater realm of receiving and giving love to God.

Professing to be wise, they became fools, and changed the glory of the incorruptible God into an image made like corruptible man—and birds and four-footed animals and creeping things. Therefore God also gave them up to uncleanness, in the lusts of their hearts, to dishonor their bodies among themselves, who exchanged the truth of God for a lie, and worshiped and served the creature rather than the Creator, who is blessed forever. Amen (Romans 1:22-25).

When we are bound by lust, we are entering into the realm of worshiping the creature rather than the Creator. When we operate by lust, we are exalting what is of the natural—whether it be a person's body, cars, money, or fame—above God. This is why the first commandment given by God on the mountain to Moses was, "I am the Lord your God who brought you out of the land of Egypt, out of the house of bondage. You shall have no other gods before Me" (Deut. 5:6-7). When satan tempted Jesus and asked the Lord to bow down to him, Jesus replied, "Get behind Me, Satan! For it is written, 'You shall worship the Lord your God, and Him only shall you serve'" (Luke 4:8). Jesus demonstrated to us what position the Father should have in our lives and what answer we should return to the devil when he wants us to lust instead of trust.

Walking Worthy

I, therefore, the prisoner of the Lord, beseech you to walk worthy of the calling with which you were called (Ephesians 4:1).

We know from studying the law of reciprocity that God only loves God; God only promotes God; God only saves God; God only responds to God. This simply means that in order for our actions to be worthy of God, there must be something within them of God that makes us worthy. In and of ourselves, we are not worthy; therefore, God must find something of His own nature and character within us to raise us to that level. God is worthy; He is worthy of all honor and all glory, but in order to give Him what He is worthy of we must receive the ability to honor and glorify Him.

We must receive an anointing from the Holy One before we can give Him the high praises He deserves.

Your heart is the genesis of the rivers of God.

Your heart is the birthplace of worship. Jesus tells us in John 7:38, "He who believes in Me, as the Scripture has said, out of his heart will flow rivers of living water." In the Hebrew Scriptures, the rivers of God flowed out of the temple in Jerusalem (Ezek. 47). Now Jesus paints the heart as the seat of worship and the genesis of God's river of love. We know that as baby Christians, we only respond out of what God has given us; our love is based on His gifts and not on who He is. Yet it is the humility of this knowledge that creates the synergy for growth in our own lives. If we recognize that we have received all we have from God, we will begin to see how extraordinary He truly is, and our love will mature. Even though it is God who initiates all worship by His blessing and impartation to us, we see from the example of the Samaritan woman at the well that God wants to be blessed. Jesus said to the woman, "Give Me a drink" (John 4:7). Before Jesus even mentioned what He had to give her, He asked her to give Him what she had in her hand. Jesus was also showing her the inadequacy of her methods. He told her, "Whoever drinks of this water will thirst again" (John 4:13). Why did Jesus tell the woman this? He wanted her to understand that what He had to give her was much better because it had a supernatural origin instead of a natural one. He wanted her to understand that only what was of God would satisfy her inner thirst, because she was created in the image and similitude of God.

When we allow the rivers of God's love to flow through us to touch God, we are accessing the rivers that flow from God's throne within us: remember, you are the temple of the Most High God. God no longer lives in a temple made by man's hands; He came to make His dwelling in the hearts of men. God's throne is in your heart, and from beneath God's throne flow the rivers of His Spirit and life, which corresponds to the eternal river that is always flowing from the throne of God. Revelation chapter 22 verses 1 and 2 tell us that there is a river of the water of life coming from the throne of God and of the Lamb. For more information on this subject, please read my book *Supply of the Spirit.*

Worship is the sound of a God-focused heart.

Worship is not the sound of instruments or the sound of an amazing choir. Worship is not based on natural talent—how well you can play an instrument, or how many people come to listen to you. These things do not impress God. Worship is releasing the sound of God from our hearts. First Samuel 16:7 tells us that even though men look at the outward appearance, it is not so with God, for God looks at the heart. He wants to know what is in a person's heart, not just what is manifesting on the outside. Remember what Jesus said in Matthew 12:34: "Out of the abundance of the heart, the mouth speaks."

Who and how you worship determines every aspect of your life. Your worship lifestyle determines how you make financial decisions. If you worship God, then you will give to God first. If you worship yourself, then you will bless yourself first. Worship dictates what you give your time to. If you worship God, then you will give time to moving the Kingdom of God forward. If you worship your job or your family, then you will spend most of your time moving your job or your family forward. It is not a question of whether God wants you to love and bless your family—of course He wants you to love and bless them. However, we must understand that we will never be able to do our job to the best of our ability, nor will we be able to bless our families like we want to, unless we put God first. When we put God first in our lives, we will find that loving others and providing for those we love is made easier. This is how we walk worthy of the calling of God: by putting Him first in all things.

The Lord preserves all who love Him, but all the wicked He will destroy (Psalm 145:20).

A HEART LIKE GOD'S

The psalms of King David demonstrate to us how we should approach God in worship. Many times David talks about God searching his heart, to make sure that his motives and intents are pure before God. This is the correct posture a believer should take before God. God is everything; we must humble ourselves under His mighty hand in order for Him to be exalted in us and through us.

> *You have put gladness in my heart, more than in the season that their grain and wine increased* (Psalm 4:7).

> *But I have trusted in Your mercy; my heart shall rejoice in Your salvation* (Psalm 13:5).

> *Therefore my heart is glad, and my glory rejoices; my flesh also will rest in hope* (Psalm 16:9).

> *You have tested my heart; You have visited me in the night; You have tried me and have found nothing; I have purposed that my mouth shall not transgress* (Psalm 17:3).

> *Let the words of my mouth and the meditation of my heart be acceptable in Your sight, O Lord, my strength and my Redeemer* (Psalm 19:14).

> *My heart is steadfast, O God, my heart is steadfast; I will sing and give praise* (Psalm 57:7).

These verses demonstrate David's perspective on his own heart. He believed that God had given him a steadfast, willing, and obedient heart. David is not only giving praise to the Lord, he is also claiming that God is enthroned on his heart. God is the center of and the most important thing in David's life. When the heart is steadfast and fixed on God, there is a confidence that shows up in a person's character that says, "I have the ability to praise You in an acceptable way, and You will respond."

> I entreated Your favor with my whole heart; be merciful to me according to Your word (Psalm 119:58).

Once again this verse demonstrates both David's confidence and his humility. David has already proclaimed to God the steadfastness of his heart. We know that David was a man after God's own heart. Basically David is telling God, "I am entreating You by Your heart within me. I am placing a demand on what You have given me." David says to God in Psalm 119:132, "Look upon me and be merciful to me, as Your custom is toward those who love Your name." We see that it is God's custom to pay attention to those who love Him. David had unlocked a principle: this is just God's automatic response to those who give back to God what God has given to them.

> Do good, O Lord, to those who are good, and to those who are upright in their hearts (Psalm 125:4).

> Search me, O God, and know my heart; try me, and know my anxieties; and see if there is any wicked way

in me, and lead me in the way everlasting (Psalm 139:23-24).

God will do good to those who manifest His goodness. It is only possible for people to manifest God's goodness if they have willingly received God's goodness in their heart, and responded to God's love in their actions. David willingly submitted to God's perusal because his desire was to be like God. He wanted whatever was not of God in his heart to be dealt with so that he could walk in the way everlasting. This was God's path—the path in which there is no death. David made it clear that the heart is where worship is created; he knew that whatever was in his heart would manifest; that is why he told God to search his heart and know his thoughts. He wanted his heart to be clean before God so that God would be able to bless God.

> *Trust in the Lord with all your heart, and lean not on your own understanding; in all your ways acknowledge Him, and He shall direct your paths* (Proverbs 3:5-6).

> *Keep my commands and live, and my law as the apple of your eye. Bind them on your fingers; write them on the tables of your heart* (Proverbs 7:2-3).

> *A sound heart is life to the body, but envy is rottenness to the bones* (Proverbs 14:30).

The heart of the righteous studies how to answer, but the mouth of the wicked pours forth evil (Proverbs 15:28).

For as he thinks in his heart, so is he. "Eat and drink!" he says to you, but his heart is not with you (Proverbs 23:7).

OUR PRIMARY FOCUS

The heart of a person reveals who that person really is. Your heart is going to reveal the real you. Christians need to remember that the first commandment of God is not to win souls (though this is very important!). The command of most importance, according to Jesus, is "You shall love the Lord your God with all your heart…" As important as winning souls is, to do so carries no real value if you are winning them into a relationship with no intimacy. When you win a soul, what kind of example are you giving them? Are you demonstrating real intimacy with God? If you are not, then you are merely converting them to religion, instead of introducing them to the living God.

> *The primary focus of man is to give God the worship He deserves.*

No one can worship God unless they worship Him in spirit and in truth. In order for this to happen, the love of God must be shed abroad in your heart by the Holy Spirit. When the sinful woman came and broke her alabaster box and poured the expensive oil over Jesus' feet, she was giving away a whole year's wages (see Luke 7:37-38). This was a real sacrifice for her. Just as David said in First Chronicles 21:24, "I will not…offer burnt offerings with that which costs me nothing," this woman was saying, "I will not worship the Lord without offering something that is very costly to me." God always responds to real sacrifice—David's burnt offering stopped the plague in Israel; the woman who offered the oil was forgiven of her many sins. In each case, a sacrifice is what captured God's attention.

> *I, the Lord, search the heart, I test the mind, even to give every man according to his ways, according to the fruit of his doings* (Jeremiah 17:10).

God knows the attitudes of the heart; God knows the value you place on His Word. God knows whether you are worshiping Him from a pure heart or not. God knows to what degree you respect, esteem, and honor His revelation in your life. Remember your love and fire for God will attract people to what you have. Love is contagious. People cannot help but be drawn to a person who loves all the time. If the people around you are not seeing you demonstrate your passion for God, you can rest assured that they will never desire to serve your God! When people look at you, can they recognize that there is a level of love in you that sets you apart?

Now may the Lord direct your hearts into the love of
God and into the patience of Christ (2 Thessalonians 3:5).

God wants our hearts to be directed into the love of God continually, so that our heart motives will always be pure. An action birthed
out of love is an action that will produce God's nature and character
in another person. God wants our hearts to be consumed with love
for Him so that our lives will be consumed with love for others.

Then I will give them one heart, and I will put a new
spirit within them, and take the stony heart out of
their flesh, and give them a heart of flesh, that they
may walk in My statutes and keep My judgments
and do them; and they shall be My people, and I will
be their God (Ezekiel 11:19-20).

GOD'S PRAISE

This people I have formed for Myself; they shall
declare My praise (Isaiah 43:21).

There is a people whom God has formed for Himself; these
people shall declare God's praise. Only God's people can praise
God and worship Him as He truly is. This shows you the heartbeat
and requirement of God. God is looking for a specific sound to

come forth from His chosen people, a sound that exemplifies Himself. It is a sound that is wrapped in the nature and character of God and is not tainted by false motives or the flesh.

> *Rejoice in the Lord, O you righteous! For praise from the upright is beautiful* (Psalm 33:1).

To whom does the psalmist speak? He addresses the righteous. *To be righteous* means to be in right standing with God. We begin to see a pattern among all the verses we have looked at. We see that the righteous, the worthy, the set apart, the chosen people of God can praise God. The Hebrew word in this verse that is translated *beautiful* is *na'veh*,[30] and it also means *suitable*. This verse is telling us that it is fitting, suitable, appropriate, and correct for the upright to praise God; it is correct; it is what God desires. Isaiah 61:10 tells us that He has clothed us with the robes of righteousness. God desires to see those He has clothed in righteousness praise Him.

> *And do not be drunk with wine, in which is dissipation; but be filled with the Spirit, speaking to one another in psalms and hymns and spiritual songs, singing and making melody in your heart to the Lord* (Ephesians 5:18-19).

Only those who are filled with the Spirit can sing psalms, hymns, and spiritual songs to the Lord. You need to remember the reason we sing in the first place. It is to minister to the Father's heart. It does not minister to the Father when we are not in the spirit. It does not touch His heart when we are lazy and will not enter freely into His presence because of offense, fear, and condemnation. James tells us that if we draw near to God, God will draw near to us. However, if we do not draw near to God, God has nothing to attract Him. God is speaking to our heart: "Get excited about Me, and I will get excited too, and make something marvelous happen for you!"

> *But when the Helper comes, whom I shall send to you*
> *from the Father, the Spirit of truth who proceeds*
> *from the Father, He will testify of Me* (John 15:26).

The Holy Spirit has an incredible ability to confirm what is of God. The Spirit always bears witness to the Word of God within you. When the Spirit of truth possesses your heart, He cannot help but to testify of the truth; He cannot help but to praise God. The Holy Spirit can testify of God's goodness because He has experiential knowledge of Him. He is intimately acquainted with God's goodness. When the Holy Spirit comes, He will begin to testify out of His own experience with God. That is why Romans tells us that the love of God has been poured out in our hearts by the Holy Spirit. When the soul became *lev* through iniquity, Jesus had to come with love and conquer death, hell, and the grave so that we could be restored to *nephish*—a heart like God's. Through love, Jesus gave us the ability to have a new heart and connect with God so that we can have a face-to-face experience with God. God is looking for a heart like God's. Only a heart that is like God's, a heart that is consecrated to God, can worship God.

> *Now his father Zacharias was filled with the Holy Spirit, and prophesied, saying: "Blessed is the Lord God of Israel, for He has visited and redeemed His people"* (Luke 1:67-68).

Only after Zacharias was filled with the Holy Spirit could he open his mouth and bless God. Remember, it was God who blessed Adam and Eve in the beginning. The spoken blessing proceeded out of God Himself, and the ability to bless can only come from the Holy Spirit, who is God, within us. Only God can bless God. Only a heart that has been restored to its original innocence in God can speak blessing over God. When Melchizedek spoke blessing over Abraham, he proclaimed, "Blessed be Abraham of God Most High." If Abraham is not *of* God Most High, finding his source and origin in God, he cannot be blessed by God Most High; God only blesses a heart like God's. Blessing an enemy falls into the place of God sowing seeds of love. By blessing our enemies, we see redemptive revelation at work in order to bring men to repentance. God sows seeds in order to redeem back to Himself what belonged to Him in the beginning.

WORSHIP IS CREATED IN THE HEART

God's desire is to recreate your heart into a heart like His. He is pressing you forward toward the goal of worshiping Him in spirit and truth. Allow the Word of God to become flesh in you as you read this book. Allow the revelation of God's praise to fill your mouth with the most excellent and high praises of God. As we realize that it is the Holy Spirit within us who is honoring, exalting, and reverencing God, we will be able to yield to Him so that God can be worshiped as He truly desires to be. As you worship God, your experiential knowledge of Him will grow, and He will occupy the throne of your heart permanently. God's blessing will begin to flow through you with even more clarity and understanding as God's love is poured out in your heart by the Holy Spirit, and all that God is and all that He has will be revealed in you as God makes you into a child after His own heart.

GWWG LOVE AND WORSHIP

MEDITATIONS OF THE HEART

- In order for God to come out of a person's mouth in confession, that person's heart must first be ignited with belief.

- You can only worship God to the degree that you allow love that has been shed abroad in your heart by the Holy Spirit to flow.

- God chose you to be face to face with God in God.

- Only what is set apart by God can praise God.

- Worship is the natural outflow of a consecrated heart.

- The genesis of worship is in the heart of a believer.

- A God-focused heart is a laser beam that splits the heavens and brings down the glory.

- If you can't win the battle in private, you won't win the battle in public.

- Your heart is the genesis of the rivers of God.

- Worship is the sound of a God-focused heart.

- The primary focus of man is to give God the worship He deserves.

CHAPTER FOUR

THE POWER OF THE ALTAR

THE FIRST ALTAR

Also for Adam and his wife the Lord God made tunics of skin, and clothed them (Genesis 3:21).

As God stepped into the Garden that day, His heart was heavy with grief. He knew already what lay behind His children—the choice that they had made; He knew what lay ahead—the dire consequences of their disobedience. The Garden was different now, its peace and safety somehow marred. God knew. A voice had marred

145

it. The voice of the enemy had been given a doorway by His son Adam. In one instant, Adam rejected the voice of his Father for another voice and separated himself from his Creator. The Father knew what Adam's choice would cost—in the end it would cost everything. God called out, "Where are you, Adam?!" Silence was the answer. Finally God heard a rustling from the bushes. There were His son and His daughter, hiding. The heaviness of the knowledge grieved the Father's heart: They were hiding from Him! Slowly, they came forward:

"I heard you coming, God . . . I was ashamed because I'm naked. So I hid." Adam kept his eyes on the ground.

Already aware of the answer, God stared at His son and questioned him quietly but sternly, "Who told you that you were naked? Did you eat of the tree, of which I commanded you not to eat?"

Suddenly Adam turned and glared bitterly at the woman standing next to him. *It was her fault*, he thought angrily to himself. Without even looking back at God, Adam spat, "The woman that *You* gave me gave me the fruit! So I ate it." At once Adam realized what he had done and hung his head. Not only had a blamed his wife, whom God had given to him, Adam had also blamed God, pinning the guilt on the One who had blessed him with everything he had.

God saw the man's shame and said nothing. He turned to the woman, who stood dejectedly, her arms wrapped tightly around her chest, as if she was in great pain. She never spoke, never looked at the man, never looked at God. Her guilt was evident. She knew what she had done. And now God was very angry at her. She was afraid. She felt trapped by what the man had said. She *had* listened to the snake. She *had* given Adam the fruit. And now she must face God's wrath. Yet, as God spoke to her, she did not feel anger flowing from Him in her direction. The only thing she felt was His grief. The knowledge of His grief broke her heart.

"What is this that you have done?" God's voice was deep and dark with sorrow. She wanted to make Him understand. She knew nothing she said could change what she had done.

"The serpent deceived me, Lord. And I ate the fruit." That is all she could say.

What would God do with them? Would He wipe them out and start over? Would He punish them? The Lord stood there looking at them for a long time. The silence bore at Adam's mind. He finally glanced up at the face of his Father. So kind was that face, so gentle, so beautiful...so severe. So holy. God's eyes looked down at Adam unflinchingly. His eyes seemed to look right through Adam, as if He was searching diligently for something...someone. Adam knew: God was looking for Himself. Adam wondered silently, *Is there anything left in me of You, Father?*

Suddenly God turned his face toward the trees. He smiled gently, and as God's face broke into a wide grin, a large herd of sheep came trampling through the underbrush. They seemed to come from nowhere, yet they were all bleating gaily as God called them with His smiling eyes and mouth. As they gathered around the Father, the little sheep turned to look at the humans. The woman looked down at the sheep and wept, for she knew that they would not come to her as they once had, when she had turned to let her laughter cascade down on them. When the woman had smiled the animals had gathered joyfully to her side, nuzzling her and seeking out her gentle touch. Now they shied away from her, staring at her as if they had never seen her before. She despised what she saw in their eyes, for it was what beat in her very heart, pushing out the lovely thoughts of days past: fear. Fear choked her now, and these small animals were her mirror. Whatever it was that God had planned, she prayed for it to be over quickly.

Then something terrifying happened. It was something that no human had ever seen or experienced, something they knew God hated, for it was the very opposite of God's nature and character. Quickly and wordlessly God picked up a small spotless newborn lamb. The woman knew this lamb. It was the first born of its mother. And it was perfect, as God had created it to be. The woman watched with horror as the God of life unsheathed a short blade and slit the animal's throat. She wanted to scream. She wanted to run forward and stop death from stealing the little lamb. Why the lamb? Her head was screaming. *Why not me? The lamb is spotless. I am blemished. The lamb has done nothing wrong. I am sinful. The lamb is innocent! I am not! The lamb was obedient even unto death. What am I? I am rebellious even in the smallest requests. Take me instead, God!* Her heart cried. She stood, her great eyes welling up with tears as the blood of the lamb dripped onto the ground at the Lord's feet. The great tragedy continued as God slaughtered five lambs, pulled the skins free from the carcasses and shaped them into two tunics.

Adam looked at his wife, as God gently slid the tunic over her head, covering her nakedness. His heart was breaking as he realized what he had done. Adam knew that it was he who had uncovered her. He had allowed her to be deceived. He had not corrected her. He had not shown her the Father. As the little sheep mirrored the woman's fear, so the woman mirrored the man's sin and reminded him of his failure. He turned away, angry at himself for what he had caused: his wife's innocence and carefree laughter was gone; the lives of the little lambs, forever destroyed; his own intimate oneness with his Father, lost. And what could he ever do to make things right again? Nothing.

The powerful hand of God Almighty gripped Adam's shoulder and turned the man toward God. As the tunic fell over Adam's naked frame, he heard God speak, "See. I have covered your nakedness."

The story of man's Fall is the greatest tragedy that has ever been told. We see the destruction of so many precious things: covenant love, eternal life, breathtaking beauty, enrapturing innocence, and the peace that passes all understanding were shattered that day. Amazingly we are still feeling the effects of the first children's sin. People in the world reject their Father God every day to serve the flesh and the enemy. Yet within the story we see a very powerful truth: even amid the very first act of rebellion against God among human beings, we see God's redemptive power at work.

When we read the account of the Fall in Genesis chapter 3, we also encounter the first altar of sacrifice. The word altar is actually never used within the passage. The only indication we are given that a sacrifice took place is found in verse 21: "Also for Adam and his wife the Lord God made tunics of skin, and clothed them." Within this verse we see that, according to His grace, God slaughtered animals in order to cover the nakedness of the human beings. We see the huge sacrifice that God had to make in order to do such a thing: the God of life, the Giver of life, had to end life in order to cover the sin of His children. That day God initiated sacrifice for the purpose of covering sin.

The initiation of the altar of sacrifice becomes the cornerstone for man's dealings with God throughout the whole Bible. We see that without sacrifice there is no remission of sins (see Heb. 9:22). Starting with the first humans, proceeding through Noah, Abraham, Isaac, and Jacob, continuing with Moses, Joshua, the Judges, Samuel, Saul, and David, until the building of the Temple of Solomon, and on through the time of the kings, we see that covenant with God was always established through the shedding of blood. God initiated sacrifice in the Garden of Eden in order to set a pattern of how He wanted His children to approach Him: through blood. The blood of a firstborn, spotless lamb was required by God for man to be able to draw near to God in worship. The consummation of the principle of sacrifice occurred when God Himself sacrificed His Son on the cross in order to bring man into permanent relationship with Him. Therefore Jesus Christ became the Author and the Finisher. The Word, through whom all things were created, offered Himself as the finishing sacrifice to seal the redemptive work that would bring man back to God. In this chapter we will discuss what the altar means throughout Scripture, and how the power of the altar is still at work today, calling us to be living sacrifices to the Lord.

THE PLACE OF THE ALTAR

There are three main aspects to the altar of God: the altar itself, the sacrifice, and the fire. When we look at the story of Adam and Eve, we see all three facets: first we see God, creating the place of the altar; second, we see Him slaughtering the lambs in order to cover His children with animal skins; and third, we see the sword of fire which was placed at the entrance of the Garden, held by the cherubim, to keep the man and woman from entering there ever again. As God has designed us to be restored to the environment of the Spirit, we must expect to come in contact with all three aspects of the offering before we can enter in freely to what God has for us. The place of the altar is where Heaven invades earth. When the atmosphere, the sacrifice, and the fire come together, we see the reconciliation of man to his Creator. We see God's perfect plan for man restored, as he moves into the place of oneness with God. The place of the altar is the place where God's generosity creates willingness, and God's fire creates holiness.

Sacrifice was a huge part of worship. In fact sacrifice was the cornerstone of all worship in the Bible. There is a pattern throughout the Scriptures of men and women who have sought God, and within their lives we see some very interesting similarities. Let's start with the earliest seekers in the Bible: Cain and Abel.

Cain and Abel

You may immediately say, "What? Cain did not seek God!" I have to disagree, however. Cain did seek God. Cain sought God in a way that is very common among churchgoers today! Cain sought God in the way that pleased *Cain*, not in the way that pleased God. Let's look at the story in Genesis chapter 4:

> And in the process of time it came to pass that Cain brought an offering of the fruit of the ground to the Lord. Abel also brought of the firstborn of his flock and of their fat. And the Lord respected Abel and his offering, but He did not respect Cain and his offering. And Cain was very angry, and his countenance fell. So the Lord said to Cain, "Why are you angry? And why has your countenance fallen? If you do well, will you not be accepted? And if you do not do well, sin lies at the door. And its desire is for you, but you should rule over it" (Genesis 4:3-7).

It is important to note that Abel brought a blood sacrifice of the firstborn of his flock. Abel did not bring just any sheep from among his numbers; instead, he brought his first fruits to God. On the one hand, we need to recognize that God is not a respecter of persons.

The Bible makes this clear. On the other hand, the Bible does teach that God is a respecter of Himself. When He sees His own nature and character, He will respond. God saw His own pattern of behavior in Abel's sacrifice: first, Abel brought the first fruits of his flock; second, Abel brought it in God's timing: third, Abel brought the firstborn; fourth, He brought a blood sacrifice. Hebrews 9:22 tells us:

> *And according to the law almost all things are purified with blood, and without shedding of blood there is no remission.*

Abel followed God's example in his sacrifice to God. His sacrifice was formulated to please God, instead of being self- or need-centered. In contrast, Cain did not follow the pattern given him in the Garden. He rejected God's example and worshiped God according to his own desires and will instead. The Scripture says Cain offered a sacrifice "in the process of time." When you look at the words used in the Hebrew concerning Cain's offering, the Hebrew context and language indicate that Cain did not offer a first-fruit offering. It was not the first or the best of his crop as was modeled for him by God in the Garden. Cain brought his offering whenever he felt like it. I truly believe that God's response to the offering shows us what kind of offering Cain brought. Can you see the "God working with God" principle in action here? God will always respond to God. It is a principle of His Word, and God has never failed to perform His Word. We know that Cain did not offer a sacrifice out of pure motives. We know that Cain did not offer a first-fruits offering, because if he had, God would have responded. The first-fruits offering of the Old Covenant was symbolic of God's sacrifice of His one and only Son on the cross. God would have seen the reflection of His own nature and character and promoted Himself. We know that Cain did not offer what God required. Because we do not see a God response, we can gather that Cain's offering was not birthed out of God's nature and character.

Abel, on the other hand, brought the *bekowrah* to the Father; this word means the firstborn, to have the birthright, the firstling of a flock.[31] Abel brought his best, the firstborn of his entire flock to sacrifice before God, which symbolized Abel's livelihood and wealth. This sacrifice was a costly sacrifice, not half-hearted or self-willed. Abel's heart is what set his sacrifice apart from his brother's. In his heart he was following God's example, and as an imitator of his heavenly Father, he received a God-response.

> *God's nature emanating from God's children*
> *will always receive a God-response.*

Verses 4 and 5 of chapter 4 tell us that God "had respect" for Abel's sacrifice and that God did not "have respect" for Cain's sacrifice. We should remember that at this point, there is no documentation that God required blood. So far there had been no verbal command for a sacrifice of blood, though God had set a pattern of animal sacrifice in the Garden of Eden. Just for the sake of contrast, it is interesting to note that Adam and Eve covered themselves with fig leaves, according to Genesis 3:7, which were of the fruit of the ground. Yet God did not see the leaves as an adequate covering for the man and woman; therefore, He killed the animals and made them clothing of animal skins. We see a parallel in the verses about Cain and Abel, in that Cain brought of the fruit of the ground and was not accepted, whereas Abel brought of the firstling of his flock of sheep and was accepted by God. Yet even with this interesting parallel, there is no written commandment given by God that the man must give a blood sacrifice.

The word for *respect* in Hebrew is the word *sha'ah*, which means "to gaze at or about (properly, for help); by implication, to inspect, consider, compassionate, be nonplussed (as looking around in amazement) or bewildered."[32] The word used indicates that God saw and paid attention to Abel's sacrifice rather than Cain's. In spite of this, God spoke to Cain and told him plainly, "If you do well, you will also be accepted." It seems that God was giving him the opportunity to change his attitude. God was giving Cain the opportunity to manifest what was of God's nature and character back to God. Even in Cain, God saw something of Himself. God warned Cain that sin was crouching at the door waiting to devour him. This makes it clear that it was not Cain's brother Abel whom God respected or paid attention to. It was what God found of Himself inside of Abel that attracted Him to the man. The sacrifice is what drew the response of God, not the actual person offering it.

Remember, God is not a respecter of persons. He is a respecter of Himself! Cain could have very well changed the attitude of his heart and been accepted by God. Yet he refused, and as we know, sin was there waiting to devour him. It is interesting to me that God told Cain, "You have the ability to, and should rule over sin, instead of it ruling over you." Even in his fallen state, Cain could chose to have dominion over his flesh and do the will of the Father. It was all about the attitude of his heart and his willingness to change it.

Noah

Our second example of sacrificial praise and worship comes from the story of Noah in Genesis chapters 6 through 9. This is a very well-known story: Noah was instructed by God to build a boat, called an ark, and to put inside of it seven pairs of every clean animal and one pair of every unclean animal. Noah believed God, built the ark as he was instructed, and placed the animals in it. Then a flood came that wiped out the race of sinful man. Except for Noah, his family, and the animals with him, nothing survived the flood. When the flood waters had receded, Noah was instructed by God to leave the ark. Immediately upon leaving the ark, Noah does something that he was not instructed to do:

> *And it came to pass in the six hundred and first year,*
> *in the first month, the first day of the month, that the*
> *waters were dried up from the earth; and Noah*
> *removed the covering of the ark and looked, and*

indeed the surface of the ground was dry. And in the second month, on the twenty-seventh day of the month, the earth was dried. Then God spoke to Noah, saying, "Go out of the ark, you and your wife, and your sons and your sons' wives with you. Bring out with you every living thing of all flesh that is with you: birds and cattle and every creeping thing that creeps on the earth, so that they may abound on the earth, and be fruitful and multiply on the earth." So Noah went out, and his sons and his wife and his sons' wives with him. Every animal, every creeping thing, every bird, and whatever creeps on the earth, according to their families, went out of the ark. Then Noah built an altar to the Lord, and took of every clean animal and of every clean bird, and offered burnt offerings on the altar (Genesis 8:13-20).

This passage demonstrates to us how the fear of the Lord must be cultivated in order to worship Him correctly. Noah was 100 percent obedient in the commission that God gave to him. He built the ark correctly, to the exact measurements that God prescribed. The Bible says that Noah was a righteous man, perfect in his generation. His ears were tuned to hear and obey God's voice, to the extent that Noah waited to hear God's voice before he stepped out of the ark. It is amazing to me that Noah could be in the ark for hundreds of days, cooped up with dirty, smelly animals, and still remain completely submitted to the hand of God. Noah was able to mark the recession of the water by sending out the dove and the raven. He knew that land had appeared on the earth again. Still, he waited until God said, "Go," before he went. What do we find him doing once he has set foot on dry ground? Noah took from all of the clean animals and sacrificed them to the Lord as a burnt offering. Noah's response to God's salvation was worship. Noah feared the Lord because he knew what God was capable of. Holy fear for God drove him to worship the Lord.

Noah knew the power of God's salvation. He had experienced firsthand God's favor and love. Due to his experiential knowledge of God's salvation, Noah's automatic response was to worship the Lord. God saw that Noah was righteous and blameless and chose him out from among his brethren. God worked with Himself and saved Noah from the flood waters. Really, it is no different from each of our own experiences with God. How many times, brothers and sisters, has God saved you from the flood? As God operates in our lives to rescue us from numerous circumstances, it should become evident to us how powerful God is. He is worthy to be feared! We need to recognize the love plan that God set in motion concerning our lives before we were ever born. As Noah recognized how much God loved him, it was his natural response to offer worship to God. In fact, God did not even command Noah to worship Him. The command was not necessary as Noah experienced God's love. As his revelation of God's love grew, Noah's response to God's love became inevitable.

> *Worship is the inevitable consequence of experiencing God's love.*

If a person has a very little revelation of the love of God, it would be impossible for them to give God a powerful response. You see worship is reciprocal. God loves us. He continually demonstrates His love for us by giving us everything we need, by healing us, by correcting us, by speaking His Word over us, and in many other ways. To the degree that we choose to receive His love we are then able to love God in return. We can only love God to the degree that we are willing to receive God's love. In the life of Noah and his family, we see that Noah immediately responded to God's salvation by sacrificing to the Lord. I believe that Noah was absolutely convinced that God was great. If he was not convinced, then his response would have been shallow. We would not see his immediate obedience to the will of God, and God would not have called him righteous and blameless in his generation. The revelation that we have of God's love is actually the source of worship within us. God's love, activated on the inside of us, is what enables us to love God in the manner He deserves.

As Noah worshiped God out of the revelation he had of the love of God, Genesis 8:21-22 tell us that God smelled the fragrance of Noah's worship and received the sacrifice Noah made to Him. Because of Noah's worship, God said in His heart:

I will never again curse the ground for man's sake,

although the imagination of man's heart is evil from
his youth; nor will I again destroy every living thing
as I have done. While the earth remains, seedtime
and harvest, cold and heat, winter and summer, and
day and night, shall not cease.

Again we see God's reciprocal nature at work. As Noah worshiped, God received the worship and showered Noah with His love and mercy. Today we drink from this promise. Sacrifice stayed the judgment of God for generations to come.

In Noah, God began a restorative work. After Noah and his family came out of the ark, God spoke a blessing over them that was very similar to the blessing He spoke over Adam and Eve:

So God blessed Noah and his sons, and said to them:
"Be fruitful and multiply, and fill the earth. And the
fear of you and the dread of you shall be on every
beast of the earth, on every bird of the air, on all that
move on the earth, and on all the fish of the sea. They
are given into your hand" (Genesis 9:1-2).

These verses parallel verse 28 of Genesis chapter 1: "Then God blessed them, and God said to them, 'Be fruitful and multiply; fill the earth and subdue it; have dominion over the fish of the sea, over the birds of the air, and over every living thing that moves on the earth.'" God told both Adam and Noah to be fruitful and multiply.

The dominion that God gave to Adam was not completely restored under Noah. God's words to Noah were different, in that the animals were afraid of Noah and were delivered into his hand. With Adam, there was no mention of the animals fearing him. Adam was given dominion over every living thing, whereas Noah was not given access to the realm of dominion. God never declared that Noah should have dominion over the whole earth as He did with Adam. This is just the beginning of the restorative work that God was doing in order to bring man back to the place of perfect unity with Him, the kind of relationship that God had with man before man sinned.

God's desire was to create a doorway back into the presence of God. Eden is symbolic for the environment of the Spirit. This environment is the place where we have a Spirit-to-spirit oneness with the Father. God wanted to establish an environment through His people where His presence would dominate the scene. Of course, this was not truly made possible until Jesus came and became the Doorway. Adam was the doorway for sin to enter the world. Throughout the Old Covenant Scriptures, we see God continually working to create a people who would restore what Adam had destroyed. He cut covenant with Abraham and promised that He would bring forth a kingdom from Abraham's children. Because of the sinfulness of man's heart, however, the children of Israel were never able to be God's perfect representative on the earth; they were never able to be the doorway to God's presence, a doorway for the nations to enter through as God had created them to be. Jesus became the way, the truth, and the life: the doorway to the Father through which every person must pass in order to enter into the environment of the Spirit. We will discuss the doorway into God's presence in more detail later on in the book. For now, it is important to know that the doorway was only open to those who were in blood covenant with God. Those who entered into relationship with God through blood were able to continue the restorative work of the Father through man. There was only one way to enter, and that was through the blood.

Abraham

The life of Abraham is an interesting journey of worship. We see a man who was both chosen by God and blessed by God. Here we see the pattern of God's blessings continued: God creates Adam; God blesses Adam; God gives Adam dominion. God rescues and saves Noah; God blesses Noah; God gives all living things into Noah's hands. With Abraham we see a similar pattern, with one difference.

> Now the Lord said to Abram, "Go from your country and your kindred and your father's house to the land that I will show you. And I will make of you a great nation, and I will bless you, and make your name great, so that you will be a blessing. I will bless those who bless you, and him who curses you I will curse; and by you all the families of the earth shall bless themselves" (Genesis 12:1-3 RSV).

What intrigues me about this passage of Scripture is that God's blessing is now conditional upon an act of worship. God tells Abram, "If you will leave your father's house, and go to the place I am showing you, then I will bless you." We see the same pattern with Noah who was asked by God to build a boat 120 years before the rain came. The requests that God made to these men were no small tasks. In fact, these men may have been daunted by what God was asking them to do. It is as if God was saying, "I blessed Adam, and Adam chose to sin against Me. Now Abram must choose to obey Me in order to procure My blessing." Given that man had rejected his Father, he must return to his Father in order to be blessed by Him. And, as we know, until Jesus, no person had successfully accomplished this feat. It took a Man with a heart like God's to redeem people of iniquity to a God of holiness. In this principle we see God's reciprocal nature at work once again. God speaks His Word over man. Remember that God's Word has the power to bring itself to pass. God's reasonable expectation is that His Word will take on voice and become flesh. God's expectation is that God's Word, planted in the heart of man, will manifest His nature and character, thereby giving God something of Himself to work with. God then blesses Himself within man, bringing forth even more of His own essence. Once again, God is working with God.

In this passage, we see God working His reciprocal blessing as well. God speaks blessing over the man in order to make him a blessing to God and to others. From this place of blessing, the man is able to bless God and to bless his family. Nevertheless, without the blessing of God, it is impossible for man to bless God. He must be infused with blessing first by God before he can impart blessing to others.

Man blesses because God instills the blessing
in him.

Of course, the principle of the blessing works both ways. Because we are created in the image and similitude of God, we have the ability to create with our words. This means we also have the ability to curse. When we speak curses over our lives or another person's life, we are demonstrating who we consider to be our father. In John 8:44, Jesus said to the Pharisees, "You are of your father, the devil...." When we curse ourselves or others, we are speaking from satan's resources rather than the resources of Heaven. Satan's nature is manifesting through us and revealing who sits on the throne of our hearts. When we speak what is negative and destructive, those words are coming out of the nature of the enemy of our souls. Interestingly enough, one of the big reasons why Abram was chosen by God, according to Genesis 18:19, was that he would impart the blessings and words of God to his children. God knew that the blessing of His Word would be perpetuated through the mouth of Abraham, which was part of God's greater plan.

Immediately after God calls Abram out of his home country, we see that Abram responds to the voice of God by building an altar:

Then Abram took Sarai his wife and Lot his brother's son, and all their possessions that they had gathered, and the people whom they had acquired in Haran, and they departed to go to the land of Canaan. So they came to the land of Canaan. Abram passed through the land to the place of Shechem, as far as the terebinth tree of Moreh. And the Canaanites were then in the land. Then the Lord appeared to Abram and said, "To your descendants I will give this land." And there he built an altar to the Lord, who had appeared to him (Genesis 12:5-7).

God brought Abram to the land that He had promised to him. God showed Abram what He planned to do for his children. I believe that at this point the blessings of God became real to Abram. His revelation of who God was, His bigness and His love, grew to the place of sacrifice. Until this point we do not see Abram sacrifice to God. However, once he sees God's blessing with his own eyes, Abram immediately worships by building an altar and sacrificing to Him. In the very next verse we see Abram moving into the land that God had prepared for him. At this point, he again builds an altar to the Lord. There is a powerful progression within this story. First we see God call Abram. Abram hears His voice and responds by doing what God commands. In the process of time, Abram receives another word from the Lord. God shows Abram the land that He promised to him, and Abram worships by building an altar and sacrificing. Abram then pitches "his tent with Bethel on the west and Ai on the east"; there he spontaneously builds another altar and calls on the name of the Lord (Gen. 12:8).

1. Abram hears God's voice.
2. Abram responds and obeys.
3. Abram receives confirmation.
4. Abram sees what God is saying.
5. Abram worships out of the place of revelation.
6. Abram worships out of the place of relationship.

We see that Abram received the word of God in his heart. As a result of the word he received, Abram took action to be obedient to God. Once Abram received the revelation of God's blessings, he no longer needed to hear God's voice in order to worship Him. Abram needed no divine prompting in order to build the altar at Bethel; he just did it because he had relationship with the Most High God. Abram was thankful and knew that God was worthy. The revelation of God within Abram brought forth worship to God that was birthed out of God's nature and character.

THE ALTAR

In Bethel, Abram built an altar to the Lord to offer sacrifices to God. Abram was moved to worship God by the revelation that he had of God's faithfulness. The place of the altar is the place where we respond to the revelation that we have of who God is. When we build an altar in our lives we are setting up a response to God's goodness in our lives. We are saying that we recognize what God has done on our behalf, and on account of what He has done, we want to worship Him through sacrifice. The place of the altar did not lose its significance to Abram. In Genesis 13:3-4, we see Abram returning to the place where he had built the altar: "And he went on his journey from the South as far as Bethel, to the place where his tent had been at the beginning, between Bethel and Ai, to the place of the altar which he had made there at first. And there Abram called on the name of the Lord." Once again we see Abram worshiping the Lord and calling on Him. Why did Abram return to the place of the altar to call on the name of the Lord? Could he not have built an altar and called out to God in any place? Perhaps he could have. I believe that Abram was recognizing the word of the Lord. He was responding once again to the revelation he had received in that place. It was at Bethel that God's blessing had become a reality to Abram. The altar indicated to Abram that he had heard from God. The altar was a place of great confidence for him, for it was the place where he had had intimate communication with God and responded with worship to the revelation of God's love.

For Adam and Eve, that place was in the Garden of Eden where God's voice, presence, and power pervaded everything. Abram longed for this place. He built a prayer closet for himself in a place called Bethel where he had heard God's voice. Abram's confidence was in that place. He knew if he returned to that place, he would hear from God again. We see God's heartbeat in all of this: God wants us not only to return to the place of God's voice, power, and presence, but also to dwell in it forever. Eden is the environment of the spirit, and when we worship God by building an altar of sacrifice to Him, we are creating an atmosphere where God's voice, power, and presence will be welcome. When we say, "Here I am, Lord. I am a living sacrifice. Do with me what You desire," we are creating the place of the altar, the secret place where God's heavenly atmosphere can invade earth.

The Children of Israel

> *So the children of Israel went into the midst of the sea on the dry ground, and the waters were a wall to them on their right hand and on their left. And the Egyptians pursued and went after them into the midst of the sea, all Pharaoh's horses, his chariots, and his horsemen. Now it came to pass, in the morning watch, that the Lord looked down upon the army of the Egyptians through the pillar of fire and cloud, and He troubled the army of the Egyptians. And He took off their chariot wheels, so that they drove them with difficulty; and the Egyptians said, "Let us flee from the face of Israel, for the Lord fights for them against the Egyptians." Then the Lord said to Moses, "Stretch out your hand over the sea, that the waters*

may come back upon the Egyptians, on their chariots, and on their horsemen." And Moses stretched out his hand over the sea; and when the morning appeared, the sea returned to its full depth, while the Egyptians were fleeing into it. So the Lord overthrew the Egyptians in the midst of the sea. Then the waters returned and covered the chariots, the horsemen, and all the army of Pharaoh that came into the sea after them. Not so much as one of them remained. But the children of Israel had walked on dry land in the midst of the sea, and the waters were a wall to them on their right hand and on their left. So the Lord saved Israel that day out of the hand of the Egyptians, and Israel saw the Egyptians dead on the seashore. Thus Israel saw the great work which the Lord had done in Egypt; so the people feared the Lord, and believed the Lord and His servant Moses. Then Moses and the children of Israel sang this song to the Lord, and spoke, saying: "I will sing to the Lord, for He has triumphed gloriously! The horse and its rider He has thrown into the sea!" (Exodus 14:22-15:1)

There is a strong pattern in all of these stories which is continued throughout all of the Scriptures: God speaks His word, the people obey, God sends His salvation/blessing, and the people respond. In Exodus we see this pattern repeatedly, as God sends Moses to the Israelites in Egypt. By the mouth of Moses and Aaron, God commands Pharaoh to let His people go. Through the mouth of Moses and Aaron, God brings down plagues, in order to show His triumph over the gods of Egypt. And through the mouth of Moses and Aaron, God gives commands to the children of Israel concerning the Passover and their exodus from Egypt.

This story is distinct from the other stories we have studied so far in one regard. The difference lies in the hearts of the people. Abel, Noah, and Abraham were not perfect men, for they made mistakes and needed forgiveness and grace, yet their hearts were soft toward God. They desired to do God's will and called on the name of the Lord frequently to find out what His commands were. In contrast, the Bible tells us that the people of Israel were a stiff-necked people who constantly hardened their hearts against God. They fought against God's delegated authority (Moses), complaining and murmuring about the smallest discomforts and circumstances. The Israelites took the first opportunity to make idols and reject the leadership of God. They chafed at the yoke of the law of God, instead of seeing it as protection and love. In other words, they were a difficult people. In spite of all this, God continued to love Israel for the sake of the patriarchs, Abraham, Isaac, and Jacob. On account of the "God working with God" relationship that had been established between God and Abraham, the descendents of Abraham were blessed and protected by God even in times of great rebellion. Though God allowed sickness to kill them, snakes to bite them, fire to devour them, and many other judgments to come upon them, He used all of these circumstances to turn the hearts of the people back to Him. The wind would turn, and the people would serve Him again for a time. We see this same pattern with David and his children. David was a man after God's own heart; hence, God blessed him and promised that his sons would rule in Israel forever. Even though the sons of David were not always righteous (in fact, most of them were very wicked), God kept His word to David and blessed his children. We will discuss this more in a later chapter.

In the above Scripture passage, we see that the people of Israel experienced a great victory through God's power. The Lord split the Red Sea for them and saved them from the Egyptian army. Due to the salvation they experienced, we see an immediate response of worship offered by the Israelites to God. They sang songs to the Lord and danced before the Lord. Out of the revelation that they had of the bigness of God, a response came.

> *The Lord is my strength and song, and He has become my salvation; He is my God, and I will praise Him; My father's God, and I will exalt Him. The Lord is a man of war; The Lord is His name....Your right hand, O Lord, has become glorious in power; Your right hand, O Lord, has dashed the enemy in pieces. And in the greatness of Your excellence You have overthrown those who rose against You; You*

sent forth Your wrath; it consumed them like stubble
....You in Your mercy have led forth the people whom
You have redeemed; You have guided them in Your
strength to Your holy habitation. The people will hear
and be afraid; Sorrow will take hold of the inhabi-
tants of Philistia. Then the chiefs of Edom will be dis-
mayed; the mighty men of Moab, trembling will take
hold of them; all the inhabitants of Canaan will melt
away. Fear and dread will fall on them; by the great-
ness of Your arm they will be as still as a stone, till
Your people pass over, O Lord, till the people pass
over whom You have purchased. You will bring them
in and plant them in the mountain of Your inheri-
tance, in the place, O Lord, which You have made for
Your own dwelling, the sanctuary, O Lord, which
Your hands have established. The Lord shall reign
forever and ever (Exodus 15:2-3,6-7,13-18).

Here we see another powerful progression. There is a
prophetic foresight within these verses that shows us the purpose
and flow of worship. As the children of Israel began to worship
God for His greatness and power, they began to see down the
road. They could see that God was going to scatter their enemies
before them, and that He was going to bring them into His holy
mountain and to His holy sanctuary. As they worshiped the Lord,
their eyes were open to see the restorative work that had been set

in motion by God Himself. God would restore those who worshiped Him and who belonged to Him through covenant to the place of the environment of the spirit. God wanted to take them from Egypt, from the clutches of the enemy, to the high and holy places of the spirit.

> *It is only in the place of worship that God's prophetic destiny can be fully realized.*

Worship carries the reward of God's continual dwelling place. Worship carries us into the place of God's voice, presence, and power, and will position us for the God-given destiny that God has for us. Worship settles us in the environment of the Spirit's control. In the place of the altar, we are yielded to the hand of God, to the purposes of God, and to the vision of God. In the place of the altar, God's love plan is pushing us forward into the perfect destiny that love prepared for us before time began. God's love plan is toward love, from love, and for love: that means that He is really working in love to bring forth love's destiny through the yielded vessel you are! God wants to restore us to the place where God is walking and talking with God within us, just as the Lord did with Adam and Eve before the Fall. Take note that worship is the method through which this will be accomplished. When we release God's nature into the atmosphere by loving God back with the love that He gave us, we are altering our surroundings and making our world into a place where God's voice, presence, and power are continually present.

King David and His Son Solomon

Solomon, King David's son, was chosen by God to build His temple. The temple was to be a place where the glory of God rested. It was to be a place where the children of Israel could return when they had been rebellious against the Lord. Everything about the building of the temple was preordained by God. It was to be built on Mount Moriah, the mountain where Jesus would be crucified hundreds of years later. According to Second Chronicles 3:1, Solomon chose to build the temple in a place where God had appeared to his father David. This was a place of sacrifice where David had learned the price of worship:

> Now Solomon began to build the house of the Lord at Jerusalem on Mount Moriah, where the Lord had appeared to his father David, at the place that David had prepared on the threshing floor of Ornan the Jebusite (2 Chronicles 3:1).

To find out the significance of this threshing floor, we must go back and read the story of David and the census, located in Second Samuel chapter 24:

> And David said to Gad, "I am in great distress. Please let us fall into the hand of the Lord, for His mercies are great; but do not let me fall into the hand of man" (2 Samuel 24:14).

David had done something that had demonstrated lack of trust in the Lord: he had taken a census of the fighting men of Israel to see how many could fight in case of an attack. He knew it was wrong, was very convicted, and sought out the prophet for correction. The Lord gave him a choice: Israel would either suffer three years of famine, three months of defeat before their enemies, or three days of devouring plague. David chose the plague because he would be at the mercy of God and not at the mercy of men. This was a wise choice. Keep in mind that it was the Lord who declared that David had a heart like His. When David chose to be in God's hands rather than men's, he was declaring that he trusted in the Lord God. David was declaring that even though he had made a mistake, his heart was right before God, and he would trust in the Lord, no matter what. It was from the place of trust that David went to make a sacrifice.

So David went up at Gad's word, as the Lord commanded. And when Arau'nah looked down, he saw the king and his servants coming on toward him; and Arau'nah went forth, and did obeisance to the king with his face to the ground. And Arau'nah said, "Why has my lord the king come to his servant?" David said, "To buy the threshing floor of you, in order to build an altar to the Lord, that the plague may be averted from the people." Then Arau'nah said to David, "Let my lord the king take and offer up what seems good to him; here are the oxen for the burnt offering, and the threshing sledges and the yokes of the oxen for the wood. All this, O king, Arau'nah gives to the king." And Arau'nah said to the king, "The Lord your God accept you." But the king said to Arau'nah, "No, but I will buy it of you for a price; I will not offer burnt offerings to the Lord my God which cost me nothing." So David bought the threshing floor and the oxen for fifty shekels of silver. And David built there an altar to the Lord, and offered burnt offerings and peace offerings. So the Lord heeded supplications for the land, and the plague was averted from Israel (2 Samuel 24:19-25 RSV).

These verses are powerful because they demonstrate the willingness of David's heart to sacrifice to the Lord. David did not want to offer something to God which had cost him nothing. He knew the worthiness, the strength, the honor, and the power of his God. He knew the forgiveness that only God offered to those who served Him. You see, David's heart was to please the Lord. His heart was righteous before God. The key to David's sacrifice is that it proceeded forth out of God's heart. God is a giver. God makes the ultimate sacrifice on our behalf so that we can have intimate relationship with Him. When David chose to sacrifice what was precious to him in order to please the Father's heart, he was tapping into a New Covenant principle. John 3:16 tells us, "For God so loved the world that He gave....” God’s heart is a giving heart. When David gave a costly sacrifice on the altar to God, on behalf of His sheep, the children of Israel, God recognized His own giving and generous Spirit working in and through David; therefore, God responded and ended the plague.

> *Willingness to give is produced as a response to the revelation of God’s generosity.*

The willingness to give comes out of a heart like God’s. We see this same principle at work in Second Corinthians 8:1-5:

> *Moreover, brethren, we make known to you the grace of God bestowed on the churches of Macedonia: that in a great test of affliction the abundance of their joy and their deep poverty abounded in the riches of their liberality. For I bear witness that according to their ability, yes, and beyond their ability, they were freely willing imploring us with much urgency that we would receive the gift and the fellowship of the ministering to the saints. And not only as we had hoped, but they first gave themselves to the Lord, and then to us by the will of God.*

In this case the Macedonians were willing, above and beyond their ability in the natural, to give to the apostles what was needed by the church at Jerusalem. Understand, brothers and sisters, God's divine influence is the only reason a person can give willingly. Verse 1 tells us that it was the grace of God manifesting through the people of God that moved them to give above and beyond their ability. We know that grace is the divine influence upon the heart and its reflection in the life. As God's influence was imparted to them by Paul, the church at Macedonia was able to reflect a heart like God's in a willingness to give financially to the Kingdom of God. They were able to give to the level of such great sacrifice because the nature of a giver had been imparted to them. It is obvious that most people are not naturally prone to give away everything they have; humans are not born givers. Even so, they can become that way as God's divine influence is imparted to them, and as they reflect His nature and character in their lives.

Returning to the story of David, we see that his heart, which was like God's, was also reflected and imparted to the children of Israel under his reign.

> Then the heads of fathers' houses made their freewill offerings, as did also the leaders of the tribes, the commanders of thousands and of hundreds, and the officers over the king's work. They gave for the service of the house of God five thousand talents and ten thousand darics of gold, ten thousand talents of silver, eighteen thousand talents of bronze, and a hundred thousand talents of iron. And whoever had

precious stones gave them to the treasury of the house
of the Lord, in the care of Jehi'el the Gershonite.
Then the people rejoiced because these had given
willingly, for with a whole heart they had offered
freely to the Lord; David the king also rejoiced
greatly (1 Chronicles 29:6-9 RSV).

This passage tells us that the people of Israel gave their wealth to the house of God with a whole heart. The Hebrew word, which we translate as *whole,* is the word *shalem.* This word means complete, perfect, and whole.[33] Many people might read this passage and get the impression that the Israelites were bringing an offering with great enthusiasm. When a person uses the phrase, "with my whole heart," that is usually what they mean. They are accomplishing something with all the ability that they have within themselves. They are giving themselves wholeheartedly to the doing of it. All of this might be true of the Israelites: I am sure that they were very enthusiastic and that they gave themselves to the work wholeheartedly. The word *shalem,* however, does not actually mean to be enthusiastic or wholehearted. The implication of this word is that, when the Israelites brought their freewill offering, they were no longer operating in a heart of iniquity. The picture we get from the original text is that they had been given a "whole" or perfect heart from which they could offer God the kind of sacrifice that He deserved. This is a picture of the restoration God desires every person to experience: He wants us to trade in a heart of iniquity for a heart like God's. The heart of innocence that draws its breath from God and can give God the worship that He deserves is a heart that reflects God's nature and character perfectly. Once again this story is really expressing God's heart to restore us to the environment of the Spirit, to take us back to Eden, the secret place, the place of God's voice, power, and presence. As the children of Israel brought their gifts to God's altar, they were able to operate in the innocent heart of God, creating a place that was ripe for God's glory.

Purity of heart and motive are absolutely essential for the expression of true worship.

Who may ascend into the hill of the Lord? Or who may stand in His holy place? He who has clean hands and a pure heart, who has not lifted up his soul to an idol, nor sworn deceitfully. He shall receive blessing from the Lord, and righteousness from the God of his salvation (Psalm 24:3-5).

What is acceptable in the presence of God? Only what is of God is truly acceptable to Him. God will settle for nothing less than a people who look, act, and talk just like Him. The ability to worship God as the children of Israel did, offering God their finances, time, energy, and resources willingly without holding back, does not proceed out of the heart of iniquity, or out of sinful man. Worship such as this can only come out of a heart like God's.

True worship proceeds out of the revelation of God within God's chosen people toward God.

> *But who am I, and who are my people, that we should be able to offer so willingly as this? For all things come from You, and of Your own we have given You....O Lord our God, all this abundance that we have prepared to build You a house for Your holy name is from Your hand, and is all Your own* (1 Chronicles 29:14,16).

David makes it clear in this passage: I can do nothing, nor is anything I have really mine. The only ability I have is to give willingly all that I receive from the Lord, for He is the One who gave it to me under stewardship. David is basically saying, "I choose to give to God what belongs to Him." Worship that is birthed from the resources of God within us will be acceptable to God. We must give to God on the altar what belongs to Him already, holding nothing back.

THE ALTAR OF ELIJAH

Throughout Old Testament times, God often revealed Himself as the God of fire. In Malachi He is compared to a refiner of gold and silver. Under the Old Covenant, fire symbolized sanctification and purging. Fire symbolized God's power poured out on humans, either as judgment or as favor. Fire is what separated

God's people from the nations of the world. In the story of Abraham, God cut covenant with a man by walking between the halves of the sacrifice in a pillar of fire. It was the God of Abraham who showered down fire on the cities of Sodom and Gomorrah. God appeared to Moses in a burning bush and sent Him to deliver Israel from the hands of the Egyptians. For the children of Israel, God was a pillar of cloud by day, and a pillar of fire by night. When the Egyptians came against them, God stood between Israel and the Egyptians as a pillar of fire. On Mount Sinai, God covered the mountain with fire and smoke and appeared to Moses from the fire. Exodus 24:17 tells us that the sight of the glory of the Lord was like a great devouring fire. The fire of the Lord consumed Gideon's offering, rising miraculously out of a rock. In the building of the temple of Solomon, God answered with fire and consumed the sacrifices that Solomon offered on the altar. Here we see God's covenant people crying out to God and God answering with fire. In Ezekiel, the Lord appeared as a man of fire from the loins down and fire from the loins up (see Ezek. 1:27). In Jeremiah, God's word was like a fire shut up in His bones, a fire that burns up all the chaff.

It is apparent that God made His power known through fire. His power manifested many times as fire. I believe one of the most compelling examples of this lies in the story of Elijah. Within this story we see a very clear New Covenant parallel. The story of Elijah paints a strong picture for us of how God responds to God, and what our role is as God's covenant people.

Then Elijah said to the people, "I alone am left a prophet of the Lord; but Baal's prophets are four hundred and fifty men. Therefore let them give us two bulls; and let them choose one bull for themselves, cut it in pieces, and lay it on the wood, but put no fire under it; and I will prepare the other bull, and lay it on the wood, but put no fire under it. Then you call on the name of your gods, and I will call on the name of the Lord; and the God who answers by fire, He is God." So all the people answered and said, "It is well spoken" (1 Kings 18:22-24).

We need to remember that Elijah knew God. He knew the power of the Lord perhaps better than anyone else in the land at that time. He knew God's covenant principles. When Elijah placed this challenge before the prophets of Baal, he must have realized already what the outcome would be. Throughout the Old Testament, the God of Israel had always answered with fire. If God refused to do so now, it would go against God's very nature and character. Well, we all know the story. The prophets of Baal cried out to their gods, but received no answer. Elijah mocked and made fun of them, to the point that they began to cut themselves in order to procure an answer from their idols. And of course their gods were unable to answer with fire.

And Elijah took twelve stones, according to the number of the tribes of the sons of Jacob, to whom the word of the Lord had come, saying, "Israel shall be your name." Then with the stones he built an altar in the name of the Lord; and he made a trench around the altar large enough to hold two seahs of seed. And he put the wood in order, cut the bull in pieces, and laid it on the wood, and said, "Fill four waterpots with water, and pour it on the burnt sacrifice and on the wood." Then he said, "Do it a second time," and they did it a second time; and he said, "Do it a third time," and they did it a third time. So the water ran all around the altar; and he also filled the trench with water. And it came to pass, at the time of the offering of the evening sacrifice, that Elijah the prophet came near and said, "Lord God of Abraham, Isaac, and Israel, let it be known this day that You are God in Israel and I am Your servant, and that I have done all these things at Your word. Hear me, O Lord, hear me, that this people may know that You are the Lord God, and that You have turned their hearts back to You again." Then the fire of the Lord fell and consumed the burnt sacrifice, and the wood and the stones and the dust, and it licked up the water that was in the trench. Now when all the people saw it, they fell on their faces; and they said, "The Lord, He is God! The Lord, He is God!" (1 Kings 18:31-39)

When we look at this story with a focus on the reciprocal nature of God, we see God's character revealed in a step-by-step pattern. First, Elijah builds the place of the altar, ensuring that God's nature and character will be revealed even in its construction. Elijah uses twelve stones to build the altar, the number of the sons of Israel. In this passage, the man of God reminds the Lord of His word: "Israel shall be your name." Why was this detail added? It seems unimportant to the story at first glance, but as we dig deeper, we find out that Elijah was calculating his worship for a God response. Remember that God told Moses, "I am the God of Abraham, the God of Isaac, and the God of Jacob." God identified Himself with Abraham and his seed after him, declaring that He was their God by blood covenant. As Elijah built his altar, he was reminding God, "Remember, Lord, you said you were the God of Israel. These are Your covenant people—Your chosen ones! What are You willing to do to turn their hearts back to You?" Keep in mind, as we look at this story carefully, that God only works with God. Can you see to what extent Elijah went to demonstrate God's nature and character back to God? This was the key to the God response.

Not only did Elijah remind God of His covenant, He also reminded God of the nation that He had chosen for Himself. In all these examples, Elijah is putting God in remembrance of His covenant word. The man of God even uses such phrases as, "to whom the word of the Lord had come," and "according to the word of the Lord." Elijah claims, "It's not me who is at stake here, Lord! It's Your word." Elijah has water poured out on top of the sacrifice three times. The water could symbolize many things, yet I truly believe it symbolizes God's provision for the children of Israel. Elijah is reminding God that the Lord's steadfast covenant love never ceases. He is reminding God that, even though the children of Israel were in disobedience to Him, they are still His chosen people. It had always been the mighty hand of God that had turned His children back to Him in times past. Elijah was asking God to move on behalf of His children again, and to bring them back to Him.

Elijah, set on receiving a God response, does not merely end his cry to God there. Elijah decides to remind God of his own obedience as well. Elijah cries out, "I have been obedient to Your word, Lord!" Elijah claims that, even if the children of Israel have been disobedient and not kept God's word, Elijah should still receive a God response because he has loved God's word and kept it. Elijah refuses to settle for anything less than all that God is and all that God has. Elijah also makes his purpose very clear—that the people may know that the Lord is God, and that their hearts would be turned back to the Lord. The man of God declares that he is operating in the heart of God, and that his desires line up with God's desires. Elijah is reminding God that he and the Lord are in unity, walking in agreement, and that for this reason alone, God should answer him.

What a powerful story of God's reciprocal nature! Elijah is coming to God, not as a man, but as God's chosen vessel, claiming to represent accurately God's word to God, and giving back to God what belongs to Him, for the purpose of turning the hearts of God's covenant children. This is a divine setup. Elijah knew what it would take to receive a God response; the man of God knew that only God can move the hand of God. Therefore, Elijah did not bring a sacrifice made and chosen by human hands or minds; instead, he brought God's children before His face to remind God of who He is and what He has done in the past for the sake of His covenant. God is God, and there is no other! What belongs to God is God's, and He will share it with no other. God will do whatever it takes to redeem what is of God, to rescue what belongs to Him, and to intervene on behalf of Himself.

Within this story we see all three aspects of the place of the altar: first of all, Elijah builds an altar, creating an atmosphere based on God's principles. Elijah even waits until the appropriate time to offer the sacrifices. The man of God uses the correct amount of stones to build the altar, even as Aaron, the High Priest of God, carried the names of the twelve tribes of Israel under his ephod, in order to remind God of His covenant people. Elijah is yielded and one with God in his heart, words, and actions; he is walking in the place of agreement with God's principles. Second, the sacrifice is present; Elijah slaughtered a bull to offer to the Lord. And I would also like to point out that Elijah's life was a sacrifice to the Lord, holy and acceptable. Third, God responded to the word of God and to the holy sacrifice with the fire of God. We see within this story a prototype of the Trinity, the Godhead, manifesting in glory on the earth: we see God the Father in Heaven; we see the Word of God, as spoken through the mouth of the prophet;

and we see the prototype of the Holy Spirit as the fire of God, God's answer to the altar and the sacrifice.

THE ALTAR OF GOD

The God we serve is not like the gods of the nations. The Scriptures teach us that the Lord is not like an idol made by human hands, which cannot speak (see Ps. 135:15-16). The gods of the nations were fashioned to be super-humans, having supernatural powers, yet retaining the human failures and weaknesses found on earth. These gods were not holy because their standard was the lifestyle of those who served them. The gods of the nations had men as their prototype. It is not so with the God of the Scriptures. The Lord God expects that humans attain to His standard. And, in order to have relationship with Him, the requirement is to become like Him.

God's presence is holiness, and there is only one way to get to His presence. Jesus is the door. Jesus said, "I am the way, the truth, and the life. No one comes to the Father except through Me" (John 14:6).

Jesus, Immanuel, God with us, is the only way to God.

David claimed that the only way to worship God was to give God what was of His own, what proceeded from Him, and what belonged to Him already (see 1 Chron. 29:14-16). Jesus is reiterating this truth by telling us that the only way to worship God is to approach God through God. There is only one way to God and that is through the cross of Jesus Christ. That is why everything we do is done in the name of Jesus Christ. Jesus Christ is the name that God exalted. According to Philippians 2:9, God has given Jesus the name which is above every name. Given that Jesus perfectly conformed to the image of God, submitting Himself completely to the will of the Father, the name of Jesus symbolizes unity with God in every facet. God will respond to the name of Jesus, because God can only respond to what is in perfect unity with His plan, purpose, vision, and will. In the name of Jesus Christ we cast devils out and heal the sick. Why? We speak His name because God knows God, and God will respond to God. In Jesus we see the place of the altar being established. Wherever Jesus went, He would establish an atmosphere where God's voice, power, and presence were always active and activating the people around Him.

Jesus told His disciples in Matthew 18:20, "For where two or three are gathered in My name, there I am in the midst of them." God wants us to be found in Christ and to abide in the Son as the Son abides in the Father. When we do this, God will recognize God and use us to perform mighty signs and wonders. If I am in the name of Jesus Christ, and another believer is in the name of Jesus Christ, we are both in God, and we will have a spirit-to-spirit relationship where God is in agreement with God. As First John 5:14 tells us, "Now this is the confidence that we have in Him, that if we ask anything according to His will, He hears us." If I am in Jesus' name, and you are in Jesus' name, God will be working with God, and we will have confidence that we are in agreement with God's perfect will. Our confidence is in God as we ask that God perform His Word, while the Spirit of God in me is in agreement with the Spirit of God in you! From this place, we experience powerful supernatural manifestations. When Peter abided in Christ, he was able to cast shadows and emanate the anointing which removed burdens and destroyed demonic yokes. Everywhere Peter's shadow fell, people were healed because Peter had found the place in the Spirit where God is in agreement with God. God has called us to be a living sacrifice, holy and acceptable. We must "let this mind be in us" which was also in Christ Jesus (Phil. 2:5-6). Jesus submitted to the will of His Father even to the point of death and beyond. As we lay down our lives as living sacrifices, we will be manifesting the nature of the Son, and we will experience the favor of the Father.

A good example of the place of the altar within the life of Jesus is when Jesus went to be baptized by John in the Jordan River. At this point we see Jesus completely yielding Himself to God's will, laying His life down on the altar for the purposes of God. He told John, "Permit it to be so now, for thus it is fitting for us to fulfill all righteousness" (Matt. 3:15). Jesus was driven to be the manifestation of Heaven's King on earth. At the baptism of Jesus, we see the Spirit of God descending like a dove instead of fire falling from heaven to consume the sacrifice, as we saw in the Old Testament. Jesus had no need for fire, because He was pure and without sin.

Fire was used as a typology in the Old Testament of God purging the sins of men (see Mal. 3:2-3). Jesus perfectly reflected the image of the Father and did not need to be purged from sin. Therefore, the Holy Spirit descended upon Him like a dove, to authenticate what was done in accordance to the law of God. An aspect of Jesus' honor toward His Father is seen in this picture. God with us, the Word of God become flesh, yielded Himself up to the perfect will of the Father God in Heaven. In response, God sent Holy Spirit from Heaven to confirm God in the flesh. Without the confirmation of the Holy Spirit, we would not see the confirmation of Christ, His sacrifice, and fragrance, which is a sweet-smelling aroma that is pleasing to God. Jesus was the Lamb slain before the foundations of the world; even so, without the confirmation of the Holy Spirit, Jesus would not have been able to produce the fragrance of the anointing that permeated and emanated from His selfless, sacrificial life.

> *Now thanks be to God who always leads us in triumph in Christ, and through us diffuses the fragrance of His knowledge in every place. For we are to God the fragrance of Christ among those who are being saved and among those who are perishing* (2 Corinthians 2:14-15).

God has called us to be a living sacrifice, holy and acceptable, which is our reasonable worship (see Rom. 12:1). God does not just want us to die to self, to the flesh, and to the power of the enemy. He wants us to be set on fire—the fire of the Holy Spirit! He wants us to die to the flesh, and He wants us to live and to release the fragrance of Christ and His anointing wherever we go and in whatever we are doing. Remember what Paul told the Romans: if the same Spirit who raised Christ from the dead dwells in you, then He who raised Jesus from the dead will also quicken your mortal body (see Rom. 8:11). We must consider ourselves dead to the world and alive to Christ. That is why Jesus said, "God is Spirit, and those who worship Him must worship in spirit and truth" (John 4:24). The Father is looking for Himself: the Spirit of God and the truth, the Word of God become flesh, Jesus Christ! When we worship Him, we must allow the Spirit of God to rest upon the Word of God and bring forth the fragrance of the anointing. Paul told the Galatians that he labored in birth pangs until Christ was formed in them (see Gal. 4:19). Paul wanted them, not only to be living sacrifices, but to emanate the anointing of God; Paul wanted them to be a conduit for the fire of the Holy Spirit. For this reason, Jesus instructed His disciples to wait in Jerusalem until they had received power from on high. Jesus shed His blood in order to cut a covenant of blood with the Father. God cut covenant with Himself that day, a covenant that, through the last Adam, restored mankind to its created purpose. Jesus Himself knew that until that sacrifice had been sealed with fire, God's full purposes and plans would not be brought to fruition. He knew that He must set the sacrifice on fire in order for the fragrance to be released—that fragrance that pleased the Father so much, the fragrance of His power.

For this reason, we say that the place of the altar is where Heaven invades earth. The place of the altar is the place where the Godhead bodily manifests in all His glory on the earth. The place of the altar is the place where God in Heaven becomes one with God on earth. Jesus prayed, "Your kingdom come. Your will be done on earth as it is in heaven" (Luke 11:2). Many people have wondered why Jesus breathed on the disciples before He returned to Heaven. I have even heard people say that when Jesus left the earth, this was the only period of time when God was completely absent from the earth. I must disagree. God's breath was still present. God's breath which propels His Word had been imparted to the disciples by Jesus Himself. I am convinced that He was breathing into them the Word of God. Jesus knew that the Father would only respond to what He saw of Himself within the disciples. With the breath of God upon their lives, they could accurately represent Jesus Christ. And as the Body of Christ drew together as one heart and as one soul, they sought the face of God with diligence, fasting, and prayer, awaiting the outpouring of the Holy Spirit. God recognized in those first 120 disciples the same elements that He had recognized in Jesus on the day He was baptized: the place of the altar, a place of unity and yieldedness to the Father, and the breath of the Lamb, the very Word of God become flesh, were present in the upper room on the day of Pentecost. And on that day, God met God. God in Heaven responded to God on earth, and the two became one.

Mercy and truth have met together; righteousness and peace have kissed. Truth shall spring out of the earth, and righteousness shall look down from heaven. Yes, the Lord will give what is good; and our land will yield its increase. Righteousness will go before Him, and shall make His footsteps our pathway (Psalm 85:10-13).

Do you see that on the day of Pentecost, the Father, the Son, and the Holy Spirit were present working together, as they did on the day God created the heavens and the earth, to bring forth a people, a new creation? God's Word, living and breathing on the inside of the disciples, was worshiping the Father in Heaven. The Father recognized Jesus, the One whom He had exalted, within the disciples, and He sent the promised Holy Spirit upon them as He did on Jesus. He was confirming that His breath and His Word were alive and well within those whom He had chosen by answering with fire, as He did on Mount Carmel when Elijah called upon His name. God recognized the covenant He had cut through His Son Jesus Christ. And as we know, the covenant people have the right to call on the covenant God. Fittingly, He answered with fire, the fire of the Holy Spirit. The fire consumed the sacrifice, bringing forth the fragrance of God's anointing. In that moment, all three members of the Godhead were actively bringing forth Christ, as They did in the very beginning.

God desires for us to build an altar in our hearts, in our homes, and in our workplaces. God wants for us to worship Him, offering to Him the worship He deserves. God wants us to worship Him in spirit and truth, so that He can respond in even greater measure. God is hungry for God! God wants to make His footsteps our pathway, so that we can walk together in agreement. How can two walk together unless they agree? (see Amos 3:3). Or how can two be yoked together if they are not in unity? They cannot. God jealously desires to bring forth God in our lives. We must receive the Word of God that He is proclaiming over our lives. We must yield to the breath and the Word of God. We must become a living sacrifice, holy and acceptable to the Lord, so that His fire, the power of the Holy Spirit, and the Anointed One and His anointing, will rise within us, consuming us from the inside out.

HOLY AND ACCEPTABLE

It is interesting that the further we get from the Garden of Eden, the less we see of the true heart of God. In the beginning man saw God face to face. After the Fall, God still spoke to man in an audible voice and even appeared to those who sought Him. By the time of Solomon, God's voice, His power, and His presence were confined to a building called the temple. In fact, to hear from God, a person had to go to the priest. No one was allowed in the Most Holy Place, except for the High Priest. His access was limited to once a year. Men's hearts moved further and further away from God's goal. Even in the midst of great separation from God, we do encounter those who sought the face of God and found Him. One was David, who, though not of the tribe of Levi, would wear an ephod and inquire of the Lord without the assistance of the High Priest. David would take a stool and sit in the Holy Place before the ark of the covenant. Solomon, David's son, also sought God, and heard God's voice clearly, as well as Isaiah, Jeremiah, Ezekiel, and Daniel, the great prophets of the Old Covenant. Anyone who was willing was able to meet God. The question was whether or not a person was willing to create the place of the altar, the environment of the spirit where God's voice, presence, and power were welcome at all times. Those who demonstrated God's nature and character before God and toward God always attracted God's presence in their lives. As the world moved further away from God's heartbeat, those who belonged to God continued to seek Him and find Him.

We are no longer under Old Covenant principles; we no longer offer blood sacrifices as a result of what God did for us through the blood of Jesus. Stepping into the New Covenant does not negate the power of sacrifice, nor the call of the believer to be a living sacrifice unto God. The principles of covenant, sacrifice, and promise were established by God long before the law was written by Moses. Abel lived before the law of God was given. Abraham, Isaac, Jacob, Enoch, and Noah also lived before the law was given through Moses. They all did one act in common: they sacrificed what was dear to them on the altar of God. The law was created as a plumb line of righteousness, yet the principles of God's covenant were written in the hearts of men since their creation.

All those who have sought God through the ages have offered sacrifices to Him. They recognized that God was worthy of more than what they could offer to Him, so they offered to Him the best of what they had. David said, "I will not . . . offer burnt offerings with that which costs me nothing" (1 Chron. 21:24). Solomon, hungry for God, slaughtered thousands of animals and gained an audience with the King of glory. According to Second Chronicles 5:6, at the dedication of the temple, Solomon and the elders of the children of Israel offered sacrifices of oxen and sheep that could not be counted or numbered for the multitude. They sacrificed because God was worthy; they sacrificed to please Him; they sacrificed to love and worship Him. Their hearts were right; God heard their cry and answered with glory.

As we approach God to worship Him, we must remember that God is seeking those who will worship Him in spirit and truth. God is looking for God; He is seeking God, jealously desiring more and more of Himself. As we create the place of the altar, coming into unity with His desires, plans, and purposes, and as we yield ourselves as living sacrifices we will see God answer with fire; the power of the Holy Spirit will begin to multiply within us, manifesting in even greater ways. We will begin to experience more and more of God's immutable power as signs and wonders begin to come forth from the place of the altar. We will see a greater move of God's Spirit among His people, as they learn to worship God through acts of sacrifice and by becoming one with Him in spirit, soul, and body. This should be our goal in worship and our focus in life: to present our bodies as a living sacrifice, holy and acceptable to God, which is our reasonable worship; that we would not be conformed to this world, but transformed by the renewing of our minds, that we may be able to prove what is that good and acceptable and perfect will of God (see Rom. 12:1-2).

GWWG LOVE AND WORSHIP

MEDITATIONS OF THE HEART

- God's nature emanating from God's children will always receive a God-response.

- Worship is the inevitable consequence of experiencing God's love.

- Man blesses because God instills the blessing in him.

- It is only in the place of worship that God's prophetic destiny can be fully realized.

- Willingness to give is produced as a response to God's generosity.

- Purity of heart and motive are absolutely essential for the expression of true worship.

- Jesus, Immanuel, God with us, is the only way to God.

CHAPTER FIVE

WILL YOU RESPOND?

THE RESPONSIBILITY OF RESPONSE

Many Christians ask themselves, "What is my responsibility toward God? What does He expect from me? I know that He is sovereign. I know that He can only work with His own nature and character. I know that I can only love God to the degree that His love has been shed abroad in my heart by the Holy Spirit. What is my part in seeing God's Word come to pass in my life?" This chapter is going to deal with this subject in detail. It is my belief that once you have read this material, you will understand what God's expectation is of you as a worshiper of God.

> *Then Solomon, and all the assembly with him, went to*
> *the high place that was at Gibeon; for the tabernacle*

of meeting with God was there, which Moses the servant of the Lord had made in the wilderness. But David had brought up the ark of God from Kirjath Jearim to the place David had prepared for it, for he had pitched a tent for it at Jerusalem. Now the bronze altar that Bezalel the son of Uri, the son of Hur, had made, he put before the tabernacle of the Lord; Solomon and the assembly sought Him there. And Solomon went up there to the bronze altar before the Lord, which was at the tabernacle of meeting, and offered a thousand burnt offerings on it. On that night God appeared to Solomon, and said to him, "Ask! What shall I give you?" And Solomon said to God: "You have shown great mercy to David my father, and have made me king in his place. Now, O Lord God, let Your promise to David my father be established, for You have made me king over a people like the dust of the earth in multitude. Now give me wisdom and knowledge, that I may go out and come in before this people; for who can judge this great people of Yours?" Then God said to Solomon: "Because this was in your heart and you have not asked riches or wealth or honor or the life of your enemies, nor have you asked long life—but have asked wisdom and knowledge for yourself, that you may judge My people over whom I have made you

king—wisdom and knowledge are granted to you;
and I will give you riches and wealth and honor, such
as none of the kings have had who were before you,
nor shall any after you have the like" (2 Chronicles
1:3-12).

When Solomon made a real sacrifice to God—one thousand
burnt offerings is no small sacrifice—God answered and
responded to Solomon's gift. If a person studied about the
process of sacrifice under the Old Covenant, he or she would discover that offering an animal on the altar took time. It was done
well and accurately, not quickly. The offering of one thousand
burnt sacrifices would have taken an extended amount of time to
accomplish, not just a few short hours. The Bible does not actually say how long Solomon and the assembly were on the mountain seeking the Lord; however, we can surmise that it was days,
perhaps weeks, that they dedicated to God's presence. At the end
of this period of time, God showed up in a very powerful and
unprecedented way to King Solomon. As we discussed in Chapter
Two, the ability to give God praise and worship comes from the
Holy Spirit within us who testifies continually of God's goodness
and mighty works. That is why we know that it would be impossible for Solomon to offer his sacrifice of his own volition. Solomon
was responding to the goodness of God which he had seen
demonstrated throughout the life of his father, David, and in his
own life.

HAVING EYES TO SEE

Our first responsibility before God is to recognize what God has accomplished on our behalf. Merely having the eyes to see how God has blessed us, healed us, transformed us, and set us free, comes from God alone. Paul prayed in Ephesians 1:17-18, "That the God of our Lord Jesus Christ, the Father of glory, may give to you the spirit of wisdom and revelation in the knowledge of Him, the eyes of your understanding being enlightened; that you may know what is the hope of His calling, what are the riches of the glory of His inheritance in the saints." Paul was praying that the Christians living in Ephesus would be given the ability to see and understand what God had given them in Christ. Not only had God saved them from a sinful lifestyle, but He had also delivered them from death (see 1 Cor. 15:20-28; Heb. 2:14-15; 1 Pet. 1:23-25), sickness (see Isa. 53:5; Mal. 4:2; James 5:14-15; 1 Pet. 2:24), and fear (see Ps. 27:1-3; 2 Tim. 1:7; 1 John 4:18). In exchange, He had given them His mind (see 1 Cor. 2:9-16; Phil. 2:5-11), His power (see Mark 16:17-18; Luke 10:19; Eph. 1:15-19), and His glory (see John 17:22; Rom. 2:10, 9:23; 2 Cor. 3:18). God wants us to know as well what He has given us access to through the blood of His Son.

In light of what God has done, we must respond to His lovingkindness. Only God can recognize God; when we see what God has done and is doing in our lives, we must thank God for His goodness in flooding our eyes with light.

His light is what gives us eyes to see His love.

In the above passage of Scripture, we see Solomon's willingness to respond to God. Second Chronicles 1:1 tells us that God exalted Solomon exceedingly. God had already blessed Solomon, and out of the place of blessing, Solomon recognized God and responded to His favor by making a sacrifice. Solomon did not sacrifice in just any place either. He chose the tabernacle of meeting, set up and instituted by Moses, God's chosen leader. Solomon made his sacrifice on a strategic altar in a strategic place where God had promised His presence would be (see Exod. 29:43). God heard Solomon's response to His own nature and character in the place where God's covenant promise was made. We see once again that God will respond when He finds Himself in our sacrifice.

God will respond to our sacrifice when He finds Himself in our sacrifice.

We see this same pattern at the time when Solomon built the temple for the Lord. Solomon did not casually build any sort of building for God; he chose the best location, the best materials, and the best craftsmen to erect a house for God. Solomon was wise, in that he plastered the temple with natural glory—gold, silver, bronze, and precious stones—in order to create a place where the supernatural glory of God could dwell.[34] When Solomon moved the ark of the covenant from the tabernacle of meeting to the temple in Second Chronicles 5:2-6, we see that Solomon continued to make sacrifices even as the ark was being carried on the shoulders of the priests and Levites. Solomon showed the utmost reverence for God's presence by following the instructions that God had given in the law of Moses. Solomon's obedience to the word of God and his willingness to give real sacrifices to the Lord created a doorway for God to respond to Himself. Solomon's response to God's command gave God the opportunity to show up and show off once again. Second Chronicles 5:11-14 tells us that the priests could not continue their ministry because the cloud had covered the temple, and the glory of the Lord had filled the house of God.

In the same way, we see an amazing "God working with God" relationship being built between God and Solomon through the avenue of worship. Second Chronicles 6:13 tells us that Solomon stretched out his hands and "knelt down on his knees before all the assembly of Israel." This is a very powerful picture of obeisance and humility. Solomon demonstrated to the children of Israel how the God of Heaven deserved to be worshiped by them.

> *And he said: "Lord God of Israel, there is no God in heaven or on earth like You, who keep Your covenant and mercy with Your servants who walk before You with all their hearts. You have kept what You promised Your servant David my father; You have both spoken with Your mouth and fulfilled it with Your*

hand, as it is this day. Therefore, Lord God of Israel, now keep what You promised Your servant David my father, saying, 'You shall not fail to have a man sit before Me on the throne of Israel, only if your sons take heed to their way, that they walk in My law as you have walked before Me.' And now, O Lord God of Israel, let Your word come true, which You have spoken to Your servant David....Now, my God, I pray, let Your eyes be open and let Your ears be attentive to the prayer made in this place. Now therefore, arise, O Lord God, to Your resting place, You and the ark of Your strength. Let Your priests, O Lord God, be clothed with salvation, and let Your saints rejoice in goodness. O Lord God, do not turn away the face of Your Anointed; remember the mercies of Your servant David" (2 Chronicles 6:14-17;40-42).

As Solomon prayed, he manifested what was in his heart toward God. He honored God and worshiped God from a pure heart; the Lord God was enthroned in Solomon's heart—his public acts of worship were merely demonstrating that to the people of Israel. In these verses we have both a willing heart and a strategic altar, the altar within the temple of God. As Solomon knelt before the Lord, he was not merely offering the dead animals that lay on the golden altar; the king was offering himself and the nation as an offering to God. This prayer that Solomon prayed to God in the position of humility before His people Israel is a demonstration of a "God working with God" relationship between the Father and the leader of God's people, which opened a doorway for God to move in His leadership and in His people. These verses show us how God desires for the leadership of His church to teach the congregation how to worship the Lord God. The first verse of chapter 7 tells us that, as Solomon finished praying, fire came down from heaven and consumed the offering that was on the altar before God; the glory of the Lord filled the temple, and again we see that the priests could not even enter the house of God because of the power that was manifesting there. When our hearts are right and the altar is strategic, we can expect the power of God to show up. The manifestation of the Spirit is the consequence of God in Heaven responding to God within us.

Worship is the manifestation and releasing of God's nature before God and toward God.

Worship is your very life. It very quickly becomes clear what a person worships by asking that person what they spend time and money on. Ask a person, "What is the first thing you do with your check when you get paid on Friday?" The answer will tell you what that person has invested his or her heart in. As children of God, it is important to make our lives a worship service to God. In order for God's laws of multiplication to start operating in our lives fully, we must live a life of worship to the Lord. As we see God's goodness operating in our lives, we must allow our words and actions to manifest thankfulness in response to God's faithfulness.

WHAT IS GOD SEEKING?

Christians are instructed many times in the Scripture to seek the Lord. God promises us in Proverbs 8:17 and Jeremiah 29:13 that He is found by those who seek Him with all their heart. Many times throughout Psalms and Proverbs, the writers tell us that we must seek God's face, His wisdom, knowledge, and understanding. David writes that he seeks God early and meditates on Him "in the night watches" (Ps. 63:6). Jesus, the Son of God, gives a glimpse into another perspective. Jesus tells us in Luke 19:10, "The Son of Man has come to seek and to save that which was lost." Ezekiel 34:11-16 also inform us of what God is seeking:

> *For thus says the Lord God: Behold, I, I Myself will search for My sheep, and will seek them out. As a shepherd seeks out his flock when some of his sheep have been scattered abroad, so will I seek out My sheep; and I will rescue them from all places where they have been scattered on a day of clouds and thick darkness. And I will bring them out from the peoples, and gather them from the countries, and will bring them into their own land; and I will feed them on the mountains of Israel, by the fountains, and in all the*

inhabited places of the country. I will feed them with good pasture, and upon the mountain heights of Israel shall be their pasture; there they shall lie down in good grazing land, and on fat pasture they shall feed on the mountains of Israel. I Myself will be the shepherd of My sheep, and I will make them lie down, says the Lord God. I will seek the lost, and I will bring back the strayed, and I will bind up the crippled, and I will strengthen the weak, and the fat and the strong I will watch over; I will feed them in justice (RSV).

In these verses God is seeking what belongs to Him—His sheep. God does not seek anything that does not belong to Him in the first place. We see this demonstrated by the man who hung on the cross next to Jesus. The thief said to Jesus, "Lord, remember me when You come into Your kingdom." And Jesus said to him, "Assuredly, I say to you, today you will be with Me in Paradise" (Luke 23:42-43). When the thief spoke these words, he was acknowledging Jesus as the Owner, the Landlord of his life. He was saying, "You are Lord; I belong to You and with You." Of course, Jesus' response was, "Whatever is Mine will be with Me." The man experienced salvation because he acknowledged Jesus' Lordship. Another passage from Scripture that demonstrates the principle that God rescues and saves what is of God is Isaiah 59:16:

He saw that there was no man, and wondered that there was no intercessor; therefore His own arm brought salvation for Him; and His own righteousness, it sustained Him.

God brings salvation to God, and God's own righteousness sustains God. We have to realize the truth of Isaiah 64:6: our righteousness is like filthy rags compared to God's! God is not looking for our goodness, holiness, or righteousness. Our own achievements will never be enough to attract the hand of God.

God is only attracted to His own caliber of character.

We must be clothed with the robes of *His* righteousness in order to stand righteous before Him. God is seeking God; God is attracted to God; God desires God! God jealously desires His Spirit within you to rise up and fully manifest Himself in worship to God. God will settle for no less than the fullness of His own nature and character. When you feel the strong desire to seek the face of God, remember that is the Holy One within you who is earnestly desiring the Father in Heaven. God within you is seeking God, just as God the Father is earnestly seeking God the Spirit within you. David is an excellent example of God's Spirit within a person hungering and thirsting for more and more of God in Heaven: "Lord, all my desire is before You; and my sighing is not hidden from You" (Ps. 38:9).

I want you to mark David's complete transparency before God. He hides nothing from God, nor does he hold anything back because of fear, worry, or condemnation. If you read the entirety of Psalm 38, you will find many transparent statements. David totally exposes himself before God in an unashamed fashion, telling God that his loins are inflamed, that he is feeble and broken, deaf and mute, and full of iniquity and sin! David does not fear being transparent before his God, because he knows God can see his heart whether he is transparent or not.

> When You said, "Seek My face," my heart said to You, "Your face, Lord, I will seek." Do not hide Your face from me; do not turn Your servant away in anger; You have been my help; do not leave me nor forsake me, O God of my salvation" (Psalm 27:8-9).

> As the deer pants for the water brooks, so pants my soul for You, O God. My soul thirsts for God, for the living God. When shall I come and appear before God? (Psalm 42:1-2)

> O God, You are my God; early will I seek You; my soul thirsts for You; my flesh longs for You in a dry and thirsty land where there is no water. So I have looked for You in the sanctuary, to see Your power

and Your glory. Because Your lovingkindness is better than life, my lips shall praise You (Psalm 63:1-3).

My soul longs, yes, even faints for the courts of the Lord; my heart and my flesh cry out for the living God (Psalm 84:2).

Can you see that David's heart is absolutely steadfast on a passionate pursuit of the presence of the living God? David is thoroughly addicted to the presence of God. This verse takes worship to a different place, as we see that not only David's spirit, but his soul, heart, and flesh cry out for the living God. This verse tells us that David's soul—his mind, will, and emotions—had come into perfect agreement with the Spirit of God within him. He also said his flesh cries out for the living God. Even David's body desired God; this is a man who knew what it meant to be submitted to God, spirit, soul, and body. By reading the Psalms, we can observe the meditations of David's heart. Even when David experienced difficulties, he would press through depression and discouragement to worship the Lord. He would not allow his soul and flesh to stop trusting in the living God.

Whom have I in heaven but You? And there is none upon earth that I desire besides You. My flesh and my heart fail; but God is the strength of my heart and my portion forever (Psalm 73:25-26).

Everything that David said and did flowed out of the meditations of his heart. If David had spent his time focusing on his problems, he would not have been able to worship God with the vehemence of a pure heart. David's worship flowed from a heart that was focused on the bigness of the Lord.

This passionate pursuit of God should not surprise us as believers. Anyone who has come face to face with the seeking nature of God should desire to run hard after God. God's heart is to seek and to buy back what was lost. David is merely reflecting back to God the same kind of passion that drives God to seek us and the same kind of love that God emanates toward us. David is responding to the passionate pursuit of God. God is ravished with us because He sees His own beauty and holiness in us. God is passionately in love with us, and our job as the recipients of His goodness is to respond with all of our heart, soul, mind, and strength. We are to respond by recognizing His goodness, mercy, and love; by being thankful; by praising Him for what He has done; and by loving Him for who He is.

> *Worship is the reciprocal function of salvation, because what we have received from God we are giving back to God.*

RESPONSE VERSUS REJECTION

So when Samuel rose early in the morning to meet Saul, it was told Samuel, saying, "Saul went to

Carmel, and indeed, he set up a monument for him-
self; and he has gone on around, passed by, and gone
down to Gilgal." Then Samuel went to Saul, and
Saul said to him, "Blessed are you of the Lord! I have
performed the commandment of the Lord." But
Samuel said, "What then is this bleating of the sheep
in my ears, and the lowing of the oxen which I hear?"
And Saul said, "They have brought them from the
Amalekites; for the people spared the best of the
sheep and the oxen, to sacrifice to the Lord your
God; and the rest we have utterly destroyed." Then
Samuel said to Saul, "Be quiet! And I will tell you
what the Lord said to me last night." And he said to
him, "Speak on." So Samuel said, "When you were
little in your own eyes, were you not head of the tribes
of Israel? And did not the Lord anoint you king over
Israel? Now the Lord sent you on a mission, and said,
'Go, and utterly destroy the sinners, the Amalekites,
and fight against them until they are consumed.'
Why then did you not obey the voice of the Lord?
Why did you swoop down on the spoil, and do evil in
the sight of the Lord?" And Saul said to Samuel,
"But I have obeyed the voice of the Lord, and gone on
the mission on which the Lord sent me, and brought
back Agag king of Amelek; I have utterly destroyed
the Amalekites. But the people took of the plunder,

sheep and oxen, the best of the things which should have been utterly destroyed, to sacrifice to the Lord your God in Gilgal." So Samuel said: "Has the Lord as great delight in burnt offerings and sacrifices, as in obeying the voice of the Lord? Behold, to obey is better than sacrifice, and to heed than the fat of rams. For rebellion is as the sin of witchcraft, and stubbornness is as iniquity and idolatry. Because you have rejected the word of the Lord, He also has rejected you from being king" (1 Samuel 15:12-23).

The story of Saul's reign really demonstrates the destructive power of pride. This small portion of it from First Samuel 15 is a perfect example. At the beginning of the story we see Saul set up a huge monument to himself after he fought against the Amalekites. This was a big mistake; first of all, Saul was not responsible for their victory; God's word was responsible. God spoke His word concerning the Amalekites hundreds of years earlier to Moses: He would utterly crush them for what they did to the Israelites when they first came out of Egypt (see Exod. 17:14,16). We know that God's word will never fail; that is why the victory of the Israelites against this sinful nation was inevitable. Second, Saul was setting up a monument to himself, instead of allowing God to honor him. God always honors God; if Saul had been confident of his obedience to God, then he should have expected God to bless him; there would have been no need for blowing his own horn. Third, Saul had not been completely obedient to God's command. He was partially obedient to God, and partial obedience is rebellion. We can see how pride was building in Saul: he honored himself instead of God; he took credit for what God's word accomplished (this is a principle of the spirit of Lucifer[35]); and he rebelled against God's commandment. Saul also denied his responsibility as the leader of the nation by laying the decision at the feet of his army. He told the prophet twice that the people wanted to take the spoil. He feared the opinion of the people more than he feared God.

Saul's pride was destroying him. Instead of doing things God's way, he twisted God's commandment until it suited his own desires. He tried to take the glory that belonged to God. Isaiah 42:8 tells us that God will not give His glory to another. Saul's pride was a doorway for the judgment of God to enter into his life. Pride has caused the fall of many mighty men of God in the Bible. Many men who thought they knew and loved God were overthrown and destroyed by pride. A good example of this is found in Leviticus 10:

> *Then Nadab and Abihu, the sons of Aaron, each took his censer and put fire in it, put incense on it, and offered profane fire before the Lord, which He had not commanded them. So fire went out from the Lord and devoured them, and they died before the Lord (Leviticus 10:1-2).*

These two men were called by God to serve before Him in the temple under the leadership of their father, Aaron. If they offered fire that was not commanded, then they were not obeying the laws passed down by Moses to Aaron and from Aaron to them. They were out of line with God's delegated authority, thinking they could worship God as they pleased, and not as they were instructed to do. This spirit still operates in the church today. People think they can worship God out from under God's delegated authority. They think they can do things their own way, twisting the commands of God and interpreting the Word of God in ways that do not uphold God's nature and character. They are under God's judgment and will not prosper, although God's mercy protects them to a certain extent. I have heard many people say, "It is fine for me to worship in the way I am comfortable. I do not have to do what others do in worship. I can participate as much as I want." These statements are lies. We are to worship in the ways that the Word of God commands us to worship, and with our whole hearts. It is important for God to be able to freely express Himself through us to Himself with our whole being.

Disobedience in worship will cause hindrances in ministry, in access to revelation, and in the ability to fulfill a higher calling.

The higher calling takes obedience to God into a different level. To fulfill the higher calling means you must not only worship, value, and respect the Word of God, but you must also worship, value, and respect the word of God within God's delegated leadership in the church.

Remember what Samuel told Saul: to obey is better than sacrifice. Let's say it again: to obey is better than sacrifice! Christians must understand that obedience to God in great and small is the only sacrifice that God will ever accept. It is one thing to be a hearer of the Word. Many people hear the Word of God and never allow that Word to take on voice in their lives, nor do they come to a place where they can walk out the Word in demonstration of power. The apostle James tells us in his epistle, "But be doers of the word, and not hearers only, deceiving yourselves" (James 1:22). If you are merely hearing the Word, then you are deceiving yourself at this moment; God is not impressed by your ability to hear. You must do what His Word instructs in order to receive His attention. You must demonstrate that the Word is alive in you before God will receive your worship, for God can only receive what He finds of Himself within you. Resolve in your heart right now to respond to God. Believers are called to manifest God's nature back to God fully. Worship is manifesting and releasing God's nature before God and toward God.

Praise is accepting God's performance in your life and showing gratitude for it.

Praise is our first verbal response to God. Our eyes are open to see what God has done in us, and it causes us to praise Him for His love toward us. We show gratitude for God's faithfulness by praising Him verbally. Worship is when we enter into the manifestation of His nature and character personally. At this point we are going beyond seeing into becoming. When you praise God, you are seeing who He is and what He has done. When you worship, you are reflecting who God is and what He has done back to Himself. While praise carries the idea of celebrating God in the outer court, worship moves us into a greater level of intimacy and into the Most Holy Place with God.

To praise God in times of trouble demonstrates that you believe that God's Word is true. We praise God because we have faith in God's consistency and integrity. Worship moves us past believing God's Word is true into the realm of becoming one with the Word of God and in agreement with the Word of God.

> *To praise is to build a house for God to live in.*
> *To worship is for God to move into that house.*

The Bible teaches us that God inhabits the praises of His people; worship occurs when we tabernacle with God in the place of His dwelling. We are making His heartbeat our home. Remember, in worship, we are face to face with God, and we are kissing Him. Worship is embracing God and being embraced by Him. We are releasing God's nature and character before God, and as we draw near to God, God will draw near to us.

Samuel told Saul, "Because you have rejected the word of the

Lord, the Lord has rejected you from being king" (see 1 Sam. 15:23). In the same way, we need to recognize that the word of the Lord comes through God's appointed leaders in the church. Though we know that God has an audible voice, and though He spoke in Bible times and still speaks to His children personally and with an audible voice, more often than not, God sent His word by a messenger—God used both men and women to relate His messages in both the Old and the New Testament. God sent his word through the mouth of Samuel to King Saul, and since Saul would not heed the word of the prophet, he was rejected by God. This issue also prevails in the church today. There are many people in the church who have a king's anointing. This implies that they have a great capacity to create finances for the Kingdom of Heaven. If a person has a king's anointing, then he or she is called to fuel the house of God with the abundance that God has given; we see this demonstrated by Cyrus, king of Persia, who gave all his wealth to rebuild the temple of YHWH in Jerusalem (see Ezra 1:2; 2 Chron. 36:23). If those with a king's anointing will not yield to the voice of the prophetic, then they will miss the higher calling of God and the direction that God is taking them in.

RECOGNIZING DELEGATED AUTHORITY

The higher the call of God on a person's life, the more important it is for that person to yield to God's delegated authority on the earth. When Nadab and Abihu rejected the authority of their father, Aaron, and of Moses as God's prophet, they abdicated their position of authority over the people of Israel; these two men only had a right to lead the people as long as they recognized the authority that placed them into that position (see Lev. 10:1-3). Many people who claim to be leaders in the Body of Christ have not valued and honored the authority that raised them up into that position. At the same time, if they do not honor God's word in the mouth of God's spokesperson, then God will not honor them, and their position will eventually be taken from them.

As we see in First Samuel, Saul lost his position as king over the children of Israel, God's chosen people, because he rejected God's word that was delivered by the prophet. We need to recognize that God is going to protect what belongs to Him. He will not allow a person to shepherd His flock if he or she will not honor Him. We need to remember what John the Baptist said in Matthew 3:10: "And even now the ax is laid to the root of the trees. Therefore every tree which does not bear good fruit is cut down and thrown into the fire." If those who are in leadership in the church or who have a king's anointing are living in disobedience to God's prophetic authority, they will not ultimately fulfill their prophetic destiny. This is important to remember as we enter God's house to worship Him. If our heart is not right, if we are offended or angry at our leadership, then we will miss God's heartbeat for our lives. Offense, bitterness, and rebellion hinder us from hearing and carrying out God's instructions accurately.

COMPETING VOICES

I should point out here that as God's voice lost its place of dominance in Saul's life, another voice began to take preeminence: the voice of the people. The opinion of man became Saul's strongest motivating force, controlling his decisions as a leader. When we are unable to hear God accurately, we will immediately surround ourselves with people who will agree with our rebellion and support us in our poor decisions. This happened many times throughout the history of the kings of Judah and Israel. If a king was not in agreement with God's chosen authority (namely, the prophet), then he would find false prophets and counselors who would prophesy his will instead of God's. Again, I must admit that, to our shame, this still goes on in the church. Paul pointed this out when he proclaimed:

> For the time will come when they will not endure sound doctrine, but according to their own desires, because they have itching ears, they will heap up for themselves teachers (2 Timothy 4:3).

People surround themselves with teachers who agree with their compromise and will never expect them to change. We want short messages that carry no weight and have no content, messages that make us feel good about where we are at and take no effort to understand. This is typical churchianity. Even so, it is not God. We must begin to bear fruit as a church; otherwise, God will begin to cut off the branches that are not producing for His Kingdom. If we expect God's Word to fit our lifestyles and comfort levels, how are we expecting to be intimate with God on His terms? This will never work. God's Word, given to us through the mouths of His servants, is what washes us clean so that we can enter His presence with boldness and joy. God's Word is a pivotal part of coming before God in praise and worship.

ATTRACTING THE ENEMY

Out of Saul's rejection of God's Word, there is a shift in leadership; in First Samuel 16, God sends Samuel to anoint David as king over Israel. At this point we see that the Spirit of the Lord has departed from Saul, and a distressing spirit has come to harass him. Basically we see that God allowed a distressing spirit to come and harass Saul because of his disobedience. The spirit is not of God, but it is permitted by God. The favorable hand of God has been removed from Saul's life; satan now has access to work with himself within Saul.[36] Believe me, there is plenty of the enemy to work with in this man! Just as God works with and is attracted to His nature, satan is attracted to his nature also. Satan is attracted to bitterness, unforgiveness, anger, rejection, fear, and anything that reflects who he is. When satan's nature is present in our lives, the enemy will be looking for an opportunity to work with his nature to produce more of him in us!

Then Saul was very angry, and the saying displeased him; and he said, "They have ascribed to David ten thousands, and to me they have ascribed only thousands. Now what more can he have but the kingdom?" So Saul eyed David from that day forward. And it happened on the next day that the distressing spirit from God came upon Saul, and he prophesied inside the house. So David played music with his hand, as at other times; but there was a spear in Saul's hand. And Saul cast the spear, for he said, "I will pin David to the wall!" But David escaped his presence twice. Now Saul was afraid of David, because the Lord was with him, but had departed from Saul (1 Samuel 18:8-12).

As we read this passage, we can see the seeds of satan growing in Saul. First we read in verse 8 that Saul was very angry at David's success and popularity among the people. Then we see that he was jealous and eyed David with suspicion. After that we see that Saul had a distressing spirit and was acting like a lunatic in his house. At last, we see Saul tried to commit murder by pinning David to the wall with his spear. The aftermath of his rage was a constant nagging fear that David would dethrone him. Anger, jealousy, distressing spirits, rage, murder, and fear were Saul's constant companions, and each were a doorway for the enemy to manipulate him. In contrast, First Samuel 18:14 tells us that "David behaved wisely in all his ways, and the Lord was with him." Verse 16 tells us that David had favor with the entire assembly of the people who blessed him continually. By walking out the nature of God, David was attracting the blessings of God that came through the hands of other people of God. God, through other people, was blessing wise and godly behavior in David. God caused blessing to come to God.

WORSHIP SILENCES SPIRITUAL WARFARE

In the Hebrew culture, everything a person does is worship given to someone or something. By behaving wisely and in a godly manner, David was actually worshiping God with his actions. We see this principle demonstrated by Daniel as well.

> *Then this Daniel distinguished himself above the governors and satraps, because an excellent spirit was in him; and the king gave thought to setting him over the whole realm. So the governors and satraps sought to find some charge against Daniel concerning the kingdom; but they could find no charge or fault, because he was faithful; nor was there any error or fault found in him* (Daniel 6:3-4).

Daniel did not merely worship God by praying and fasting. Daniel's very lifestyle demonstrated his love for God. The Bible tells us that he had an excellent spirit, and even when the satraps looked for something to accuse him of, they could find nothing—no error or fault. Daniel was faithful in everything he did. Why did he act this way? Daniel demonstrated that the love he had for his God made him different, set him apart, and delegated his lifestyle.

Daniel was a worshiper of God, and we see that God delivered him from the lion's den. God would not allow what was His to be destroyed. He rescued and delivered Himself within Daniel, because Daniel was continually releasing God's nature to Himself—not just in the form of worship that is most often associated with the word *worship* (songs, praise, etc.), but by living a lifestyle that brought honor and glory to God, by having an excellent spirit, and by being above reproach among his colleagues. Daniel's faithfulness and worship of God silenced the warfare that was in his life and brought him to a place of great blessing. As Daniel demonstrated God's nature and character before God and toward God, God said, "No lion is going to eat what belongs to Me!" The result was that Daniel was rescued from the lions.

Saul's lifestyle, however, demonstrated that he did not worship God in the way that God wanted to be worshiped. Because Saul did not honor God's Word, he had no love relationship with God, he was not faithful to God. While Saul was anointed king, there was a certain level of protection over his life; because of his rejection of the Word, that protection was removed. As Saul cultivated the seeds of satan, such as anger, jealousy, etc., his life began to spiral downward until he finally stooped so low as to consult with mediums and spiritists. He opened the doorway for satan to work with the seeds of anger and jealousy when he rejected the word of the Lord, and from that moment, satan was able to multiply his seeds within Saul. When the Spirit of God was upon Saul, there was divine protection placed on Saul because of this position of authority. Satan is assigned to work with what is of his nature within a person.

Many people open doorways for the enemy to attack them by allowing the seeds of satan's nature to be planted in their souls. For example, the Bible tells us that God has not given us a spirit of fear (see Rom. 8:15; 2 Tim. 1:7). Fear is not from God, but from satan. Fear is of his nature and character. When we step into fear we are stepping out of the realm of faith, out of God's realm, and into the realm of the enemy. When we do this we are opening a door for even more of the enemy's seeds to be sown in our lives. This gives satan more to work with. To counteract this, we need to yield to the grace of God (the seeds of God's influence) and uproot any seeds of the nature of satan that may be planted in our souls.

In contrast to Saul's anger, which was a manifestation of what was enthroned in Saul's heart, David was a worshiper of God. His total attitude, the way that he served his enemies and loved those who hated him, was set on honoring God. I am sure that it was obvious to David that Saul was angry and jealous of him. In spite of everything, David did not desert his position as Saul's armor bearer (see 1 Sam. 16:21), and in his steadfast loyalty to Saul, David was mirroring God's own faithfulness.

And so it was, whenever the spirit from God was upon Saul, that David would take a harp and play it with his hand. Then Saul would become refreshed and well, and the distressing spirit would depart from him (1 Samuel 16:23).

And it happened on the next day that the distressing spirit from God came upon Saul, and he prophesied inside the house. So David played music with his hand, as at other times; but there was a spear in Saul's hand. And Saul cast the spear, for he said, "I will pin David to the wall!" But David escaped his presence twice (1 Samuel 18:10-11).

The above verse says that David escaped from the presence of Saul twice. This implies that Saul had behaved in this fashion more than once; in any case, David returned to minister to this man who was no longer in God's favor. David's love relationship with God spilled over into every area of David's life, whether it was his job as armor bearer to the king, or as a soldier, or as a harp player; he was excellent in everything that he did because he worshiped God with everything he was. We can also see in the verses that Saul experienced the overflow of David's love relationship with God. David would worship the Lord, and the evil spirits would flee from the presence of the Lord. David's heart was steadfast on God; his soul pursued God, and this nature was flowing through his music toward God.

Let me reiterate again that when we worship God we are responding to what God has done for us already. Our love is responsive and is birthed out of His love. We are not the ones who should be credited with the ability to love. God is the One who loves; First John 4:19 tells us that we love God because He first loved us. He is the initiator of all love, and our ability to love God will only flow to the degree that we receive God's love. When we love God, we are giving God what belongs to God. We are releasing God to Himself. When we give what is of God to God, we can see that God will then begin to work in our situations. He is instinctively attracted to Himself. He cannot help but to move mountains and split oceans for Himself when He finds Himself within us.

God was working with His nature and character within David to produce His own love in David's situation, and the evil spirits could not remain where David was. God was, in essence, declaring, "No devil is going to hang around Me!" The devils that harassed Saul would flee as God's presence would manifest.

Love drives out darkness; worship silences
spiritual warfare.

In reality, the evil spirits were not actually leaving Saul; he merely experienced the blessing of someone else's love for and toward God. When David would leave, I believe those spirits came back to harass Saul again. Many people experience this when they attend church. They walk in and are surrounded with people who are responding wholeheartedly to God's love by giving Him thanks, praising Him for His wondrous works, and loving Him for who He is. What is actually taking place is that they have entered an atmosphere where God's Spirit is reigning, and the evil spirits that are constantly harassing them run the other direction. These people may feel free and can even worship God themselves. Yet the minute they walk out of the worship service they find themselves bound again to whatever they had been struggling with all along. These people were only experiencing the overflow of the love relationships of the people around them.

THE RESPONSE OF HOLINESS

God makes it clear that in order to approach Him in worship, we must come with "clean hands and a pure heart" (Ps. 24:4). Holiness is also an essential key to worship. Worship should be a product of the love and holiness of God within you. In Isaiah 6:1-8, we see God's holiness is the center of worship in Heaven.

> *In the year that King Uzziah died, I saw the Lord sitting on a throne, high and lifted up, and the train of His robe filled the temple. Above it stood seraphim; each one having six wings: with two he covered his face, with two he covered his feet, and with two he flew. And one cried to another and said: "Holy, holy, holy is the Lord of hosts; the whole earth is full of His*

231

glory!" And the posts of the door were shaken by the voice of him who cried out, and the house was filled with smoke. So I said: "Woe is me, for I am undone! Because I am a man of unclean lips, and I dwell in the midst of a people of unclean lips; for my eyes have seen the King, the Lord of hosts." Then one of the seraphim flew to me, having in his hand a live coal which he had taken with the tongs from the altar. And he touched my mouth with it, and said: "Behold, this has touched your lips; Your iniquity is taken away, and your sin purged." Also I heard the voice of the Lord, saying: "Whom shall I send, and who will go for Us?" Then I said, "Here am I! Send me."

This passage makes it very clear that as the seraphim encircle the throne they cry out, "Holy, holy, holy!" We may wonder why the angels do not cry out "Love!" or "Mercy!" I believe it is because as God reveals His love and mercy, His perfection shines through even stronger. God's Word commands His children to "be holy, for I am holy" (see Lev. 11:44; 1 Pet. 1:16). The command of God is to manifest His perfection in everything we do, whether it is through love, mercy, justice, compassion, or any other part of His nature and character. As we approach Him in praise and worship, we must do it in response to God's perfection within us, and not out of the resources of our own righteousness, which, the Bible tells us, are filthy rags in comparison to God's perfection. I have heard many Christians say, "Don't worry. God doesn't expect you to be perfect." This lie hinders believers from truly fulfilling the highest call of God on their lives. Jesus did not merely die to save you from hell. He died to make you a holy, set-apart, sanctified generation, a royal priesthood. In response to God's gift of Jesus' life, we must allow the Holy Spirit within us to make us holy—spirit, soul, and body. That is why Paul prayed for the believers in Thessalonica: "Now may the God of peace Himself sanctify you [make you holy] completely; and may your whole spirit, soul, and body be preserved blameless [perfect] at the coming of our Lord Jesus Christ" (1 Thess. 5:23). Paul did not want his disciples to remain in their sinful lifestyles as if God's grace had no power at all! Yet this is what many Christians believe today. Jesus also prayed for His disciples, "Sanctify them [make them holy] by Your truth. Your word is truth" (John 17:17).

I have noticed how difficult it is to worship God when a person does not feel holy. This person will only go so far into the presence of God because he or she feels dirty and unworthy. This is one of satan's primary tactics to keep us out of a place of intimacy with God. The enemy twists the truth in order to bind us to past mistakes and unholiness. The truth is that God expects holiness; Jesus is the One who came and fulfilled the righteous and holy requirement of the law so that we can trade in our filthy rags and put on His garments of righteousness. Once we have done this we have a right and privilege as children of God to come boldly into His presence, knowing that the blood of the Lamb has made a way for us. We now can respond to God's gift by manifesting the holiness of God that lives within us through His Holy Spirit. Satan knows what God's requirement is in order to enter His presence. He also knows that Jesus' blood has broken down the wall of separation between us and God. The enemy of our souls will use the small amount of knowledge a new Christian has to bind him from ever truly entering God's presence. That liar will tell a new believer, "Don't you remember what you did before you were saved? What gives you the right to enter God's presence?" Condemnation sets in, and soon that young believer is so bogged down by lies that he can hardly raise his head, let alone his hands in praise to God.

As God's children, we need to respond to God by allowing God's own holiness to manifest through us. This means accepting the holiness of Jesus as our own, acknowledging and honoring Him for what He has done for us. This is humility, which God loves:

> For thus says the High and Lofty One who inhabits eternity, whose name is Holy: "I dwell in the high and holy place, with him who has a contrite and humble spirit, to revive the spirit of the humble, and to revive the heart of the contrite ones" (Isaiah 57:15).

God makes His dwelling in the high and holy place with those who are humble. God loves the humble! This is why Jesus had so much power! He continually humbled Himself before the Father,

234

who in turn, honored the Son. Romans 1:3-4 says, "Concerning His Son Jesus Christ our Lord, who was born of the seed of David according to the flesh, and declared to be the Son of God with power according to the Spirit of holiness...." Jesus' power was in His humility and holiness. We must realize that the same principle applies to every believer! Philippians 2:5 reveals to us that we are to have the mind of Christ; this includes mindsets, manners, and attitudes, and is part of our response to the love that God has shown us. Will we allow the nature, character, and attributes of Jesus Christ to operate through us, or will we continue to believe the lies of the enemy as he binds us to our past?

In Isaiah 6, we see the prophet respond to the cleansing fire of God with a willing and obedient heart. Once God has made him clean through the fire of the altar, Isaiah readily accepts God's commission to go to the children of Israel with God's message. We see a pattern of events in Isaiah's vision that will happen to every person who ever comes face to face with God: Isaiah sees the Lord and hears the worship; Isaiah recognizes God's holiness and his own uncleanness; Isaiah repents for his sin and the sin of his people; God cleanses him from all iniquity; God commissions him to do the work of the ministry. Once people recognize God's holiness and allow God to purify them through fire, they are ready to do the will of the Father from a pure heart and with clean hands. Holiness has penetrated them and brought them to the place of obedience. The automatic response of every believer should be to go and do the perfect will of God.

Your Victory Is in Your Mouth

Our response to God's goodness in our own life is going to determine our victory in the long run. We need to understand the importance of praise and worship when it comes to claiming victory over our enemies. Remember what Genesis 49:8 says of Judah (which means *praise*): "Your hand shall be on the neck of your enemies." Praise has the ability to conquer enemies without ever facing them in battle. Remember, praise is to recount God's wondrous and mighty works.

> *And Jehoshaphat feared, and set himself to seek the Lord, and proclaimed a fast throughout all Judah* (2 Chronicles 20:3).

Just as David set his face to seek the Lord, so did Jehoshaphat, the king of Israel. God will always respond to a heart that is set toward Him. We see these principles at work in the story of King Jehoshaphat.

- Praise and worship will only be as strong as your desire to seek the Lord; praise and worship will only be as strong as your desire to please the Lord.

- Praise and worship will only be as strong as your honor and obedience to the Lord.

- Praise and worship will only be as strong as your intimacy with God.

- Praise and worship will only be as strong as your hunger for God.

Jehoshaphat did not expect God to give him the victory simply because he was the king of Judah. He knew his position gave him favor with God, yet the king was not arrogant or proud toward God. Jehoshaphat set his heart to seek God, and he consecrated the people of Judah along with him by declaring a statewide time of prayer and fasting. The king chose to create a force of holiness and praise so as to grab God's attention. He gathered all the people of Judah together in the temple in order to seek the God of Heaven for intervention. I am convinced that God looked down from Heaven on that group of thousands of people—all of whom had hungered after God in order to seek His face, had purified themselves through fasting, had humbled themselves through prayer, and had honored God through praise—and identified Himself among His people. Revival hit these people because they operated in hunger, holiness, humility, and honor. As they worshiped the Lord, a man of God stood in their midst and proclaimed:

> "Tomorrow go down against them. You will surely come up by the Ascent of Ziz, and you will find them

at the end of the brook before the Wilderness of Jeruel. You will not need to fight in this battle. Position yourselves, stand still and see the salvation of the Lord, who is with you, O Judah and Jerusalem! Do not fear or be dismayed; tomorrow go out against them, for the Lord is with you." And Jehoshaphat bowed his head with his face to the ground, and all Judah and the inhabitants of Jerusalem bowed before the Lord, worshiping the Lord. Then the Levites of the children of the Kohathites and of the children of the Korahites stood up to praise the Lord God of Israel with voices loud and high. So they rose early in the morning and went out into the Widerness of Tekoa; and as they went out, Jehoshaphat stood and said, "Hear me, O Judah and you inhabitants of Jerusalem: Believe in the Lord your God, and you shall be established; believe His prophets, and you shall prosper." And when he had consulted with the people, he appointed those who should sing to the Lord, and who should praise the beauty of holiness, as they went out before the army and were saying, "Praise the Lord, for His mercy endures forever." Now when they began to sing and to praise, the Lord set ambushes against the people of Ammon, Moab, and Mount Seir, who had come against Judah; and they were defeated (2 Chronicles 20:16-22).

In these verses, we see a powerful parallel between Jehoshaphat and Saul of First Samuel. In First Samuel 15, we read that Saul rejected the word of the Lord. In the above passage we see that Jehoshaphat believed the word of the Lord and honored God's prophet; he also taught the children of Israel to do likewise. This is a very important point. Jehoshaphat facilitated worship for his whole community and took responsibility for the encouragement and exhortation of his whole body. This king was unlike Saul, who caused division among people and was a liar and deceiver. Not only that, but Saul chose to listen to the voice of the people instead of leading the people to listen to the voice of the Lord. Saul wanted to bring honor to himself by setting up a monument to his victory; Jehoshaphat worshiped God and instructed the people to give God the praise for the victory. Saul lost the battle and his position as king; Jehoshaphat was victorious over his enemies and remained in a position of authority. We can see that Saul's response to God, His word, and His delegated authority set him up for failure and destruction, while Jehoshaphat's response set him up for blessing and promotion.

King Jehoshaphat set those who sang in front of the army. They said, "Praise the Lord, for His mercy endures forever." The Hebrew word that is translated *mercy* in this verse is *checed*, which actually means God's strong and steadfast covenant love and devotion.[37] As the worshipers sang the truth of God's strong and steadfast covenant love and devotion before the army of Israel, they were releasing God to Himself over and over again. God's love was ascending like a sweet-smelling fragrance to Himself before the face of the Father. The Israelites were putting God in remembrance of what He had already established between Himself and His people. The people of Israel were creating an atmosphere where God could walk and talk with His people once again as He did in the Garden of Eden. They were creating the parameters of God's *checed,* so that the God of *checed* would inhabit their praises. The minute that God heard the sound of His own covenant, His own love and devotion, ascending to Him from the mouths of those who belonged to Him, He reached down and delivered Himself out of the hand of all His enemies.

> *As God's people reminded God of His own nature, God responded to the sound of God pouring forth from the lips of His possession.*

God will always respond to God's principles, God's desires, God's heartbeat, and God's Word pouring out of man. God will always work with God, and in this particular situation, God essentially looked down from Heaven and said, "Hey! Nobody is going to mess with Me!" God finds Himself in worship. Worship is like a homing device to locate God. God will always show up on the scene when worshipers are worshiping and praises are being sung. God sees Himself in every person whose heart is righteous before Him. If we study the story in detail, we will see that the enemies that were united against Israel were absolutely torn apart. Complete chaos hit the camps of Israel's enemies, and they turned to destroy each other (see 2 Chron. 20:23-24). Israel did not even get their clothes dirty! All they did was respond to the *checed* of God, His strong and steadfast covenant love and devotion, which had been shown to them throughout history. Their only responsibility was to respond by praising and worshiping the God of Heaven. When we respond to God, He will cause our enemies to turn on each other and to absolutely destroy each other.

> *When our desires are God's desires and meet God's standards, God will make a way for His desire to come to pass through us.*

As King Jehoshaphat and the people of Judah hungered after God, became holy before God, humbled themselves toward God, and honored God through praise and worship, and as they responded to God's strong and steadfast covenant love and devotion, God turned to hear the sound of His heartbeat coming from His possession, and rescued Himself from His enemies.

"GIVE ME A DRINK"

God has laid a responsibility at our feet: God has called us to respond to His heart. When the Samaritan woman came to the well and encountered the Son of God, Jesus did not walk up to her and offer her what He had to give her; on the contrary, He asked something of her instead. He said to her, "Give Me a drink of water" (see

John 4:7-42). God wants us to allow the river of His love to flow out of us in order to touch Him and to minister to His heart. By responding to His love, we will be touching God with His own nature and character. There has to be a response flowing out of you toward God in order for God to give you more of Himself. What did Jesus tell the woman at the well? Those who worship the Father must worship Him in spirit and truth. God is looking for His Spirit and His Word to manifest fully in your life so that He can continue to multiply the inner workings of His Spirit within you and to make the Word of God within you become flesh. God wants us to give Him what is of the Spirit.

FESTIVALS AND OFFERINGS

Under the Old Covenant, God had set up festivals within the year for the people to come to the temple to offer sacrifices of rejoicing to the Lord. These feasts were huge celebrations in which the children of Israel would remember and respond to the hundreds of times God had saved them from the hands of their enemies. The feast of Passover was celebrated in order to commemorate when the spirit of death passed over the children of Israel in Egypt and did not kill their firstborn because of the blood of unblemished lambs. The feast of Pentecost was to celebrate the first fruits of the summer harvest, which reminded them of God's goodness in giving them a harvest. The third feast of the year was the feast of Tabernacles, when the congregation of the children of

Israel would gather in the temple and build small structures. They would stay in these structures for seven days, feasting and tabernacling with the Lord. This again was to remind them of the day when they would ever be in the Lord's presence.[38]

There were three major offerings given by the children of Israel to the Lord: the drink offering, the heave offering, and the wave offering.

> Take the provision made for a drink offering. This was not, as some have supposed, an offering of wine for the priest's consumption, for although our King James translation has named it a "drink offering," it was actually a "libation offering." The Hebrew word used here literally means "to pour out." It was an offering that was poured out before the Lord. It was not intended for man; it was presented to God.[39]

The drink offering was a remembrance of how God's Spirit enabled people to do mighty things for God, acts that they could not possibly have accomplished in the flesh. The story of David's mighty men of valor is a good example of this (see 2 Sam. 23:15-16). Three men fought their way through an entire army of Philistines in order to get David a drink of water from the well of Bethlehem. This was a supernatural act of God, done through His Spirit. Rightfully, David poured out the water to God in thanksgiving, instead of drinking it himself. David took what he knew could only be done by

God and poured it out to God. As God's children we need to remember there is no way we could even come into God's presence if it weren't for God Himself making a way. We must be thankful for God's hand of favor which brings us to a place where we can worship God in the first place.

As we worship God, something birthed within our spirit is poured out before the Father. There is an actual flow from God within us to God in Heaven. Judson Cornwall explains it quite well: "There is a flowing from him [the worshipper] to God. Love, appreciation, adoration, and worship flow from his [the worshipper's] spirit, through the Holy Spirit, into the presence of God."[40] Worship originates in God's Spirit within you.

The second offering is called the heave offering. This offering is symbolic of when a person's soul opens before God. There are many times in worship when we see people begin to weep as the presence of God moves through their spirit and begins to work on their soul. Some people laugh when they get in the presence of God because of the great joy that He gives them. Their emotions begin to manifest what is going on in their spirit, and the two come into agreement. People need to learn how to be free in the presence of God and allow their soul to heave up a blessing to God.

The third offering is the wave offering. This offering was shaking and waving the offering before God. This involved the person's body. The wave offering is symbolic of when our bodies begin to come into alignment with God's Spirit within us. At this point in worship, there will be numerous manifestations of God's power and presence. Some people shake under the power of God, while others dance or spin. *Giyl*, one of the Hebrew words for *worship*, means to spin round and is a picture of how the angels worship God in Heaven. Many times when I have had visions of angels worshiping the Father, I see them spinning violently in the air. This is a very powerful picture of complete abandonment to God.

Within the drink offering, the heave offering, and the wave offering, we see how our response to God should be in the spirit, the soul, and in the body. The drink offering is the resources of God pouring out of man's spirit. The heave offering is the response of man's soul to God's love. The wave offering is man's body breaking forth to worship God with vehemence and passion.

> *When everything of God that is in my spirit, and everything of God that is in my soul, and everything of God that is in my body come into agreement in ravished and passionate outpouring of worship to the Father, I will be allowing God to praise and worship God.*

We can see a good example of this kind of worship in David's experience with the ark of the covenant. David danced before the ark in very little clothing; he danced with all his might and worshiped God with his spirit, his soul, and his body. When David's wife Michal saw him do this, she scorned the worship of the man of God and told him he looked and acted in an inappropriate manner. The fruit of her improper behavior was physical barrenness (see 2 Sam. 6:16-23). I have noticed in several churches that lack of praise and worship in individuals' lives I have seen can bring about spiritual barrenness concerning revelation. Deuteronomy 28:2-13 tells us clearly that those who obey the voice of the Lord will be fruitful in every area of their lives. "Blessed shall you be in the city, and blessed shall you be in the country. Blessed shall be the fruit of your body, the produce of your ground and the increase of your herds, the increase of your cattle and the offspring of your flocks" (Deut. 28:3-4). The first commandment, according to Jesus, is to love the Lord your God with all your heart, mind, and strength. When we walk in love, it brings fruitfulness and abundance, because we are obeying the voice of the Lord. David told Michal, "I will play music before the Lord. And I will be even more undignified than this" (2 Sam. 6:21-22). He promised that he would worship God with all of his heart no matter what anyone thought. Michal was barren because she touched another person's intimacy and love with God. God weighs our actions and the attitude we have toward worship in the balance. He knows who is responding to His love and who is not. He is aware when we scorn others who are worshiping God freely. This attitude can bring about barrenness in our own lives. We must lay down our pride and selfishness and respond to everything that God has done for us, everything that God has given us, and everything that God is! Choose right now to magnify and praise God with your spirit, your soul, and your body. When you worship God in your spirit, soul, and body, everything that you do is formulated to please God, from thoughts, to words, to actions. Even small assignments and instructions from God become acts that are birthed out of reverence and love for God.

God has created you to be responsive to His love. When a young child receives a gift from his father, or when he becomes excited about a trip, he will always shout and jump. This is a natural response for the child. It is natural for him to respond physically and verbally to the exciting thing that is happening. I have watched over the years as my own children have grown, how they always respond when I come home from a trip. They run to meet me; they throw their arms around me and kiss me because they have missed me. Children will laugh and shout about something as simple as their father coming home from a trip. They are hungry for my love and my attention at all times, even when I have not been away for a time. Why, then, do we as adults try to quench the excitement and zeal we feel when we are in the presence of God? All we are doing is responding to our Father, the way a child responds to his or her daddy. When a person gets excited about the Lord they are really expressing thankfulness for all He has done in their lives. We must get free as the Body of Christ to respond with excitement and enthusiasm to God's love.

GWWG LOVE AND WORSHIP

MEDITATIONS OF THE HEART

- His light is what gives us eyes to see His love.

- God will respond to our sacrifice when He finds Himself in our sacrifice.

- Worship is the manifestation and releasing of God's nature before God and toward God.

- God is only attracted to His own caliber of character.

- Worship is the reciprocal function of salvation, because what we have received from God we are giving back to God.

- Disobedience in worship will cause hindrances in ministry, in access to revelation, and in the ability to fulfill a higher calling.

- Praise is accepting God's performance in your life and showing gratitude for it.

- To praise is to build a house for God to live in. To worship is for God to move into that house.

- Love drives out darkness; worship silences spiritual warfare.

- As God's people reminded God of His own nature, God responded to the sound of God pouring forth from the lips of His possession.

- When our desires are God's desires and meet God's standards, God will make a way for His desire to come to pass through us.

- When everything of God that is in my spirit, and everything of God that is in my soul, and everything of God that is in my body come into agreement in ravished and passionate outpouring of worship to the Father, I will be allowing God to praise and worship God.

JUDAH'S DESTINY

EXPRESSIONS OF PRAISE

In the Hebrew Scriptures alone, there are over 12 distinct Hebrew words describing praise and worship. There is an interesting connection between these 12 words which sets a pattern for worship in the New Testament Church: all of the words are either verbal or physical. Most of the Hebrew words for worship contain within them the implication of physical action, and some of the words are purely physical in their demonstration of praise and worship. For example, the word *yadah*, which we will discuss further in a moment, means to worship or revere with lifted hands.[41] *Strong's Dictionary* goes on to inform us that *yadah* is also a confession of thanksgiving. Suitably, the word truly means to confess thanksgiving and praise to God with your mouth while lifting up your hands to Him. Thus it is both verbal and physical.

Another good example of both the physicality and the verbal aspect of praise and worship is clearly evident in the Hebrew word, *shachah*; this word means to bow down, to prostrate; to worship. I am sure that as you read the definition, you can see a clear picture of kneeling before the Lord, and verbally singing to Him or telling Him of your love. For many people it is a natural thing to worship God both verbally and physically. Yet for others, it is difficult, because physical displays of worship lie outside of their personal comfort zones. To worship the Lord, both verbally and physically, is not an option for those who truly love Him: it is a command!

> *Oh come, let us worship and bow down; let us kneel before the Lord our Maker. For He is our God, and we are the people of His pasture, and the sheep of His hand…* (Psalm 95:6-7).

> *Praise the Lord! Praise God in His sanctuary; praise Him in His mighty firmament! Praise Him for His mighty acts; praise Him according to His excellent greatness! Praise Him with the sound of the trumpet; praise Him with the lute and harp! Praise Him with the timbrel and dance; praise Him with stringed instruments and flutes! Praise Him*

with loud cymbals; praise Him with clashing cymbals! Let everything that has breath praise the Lord. Praise the Lord! (Psalm 150)

And that the Gentiles might glorify God for His mercy, as it is written: "For this reason I will confess to You among the Gentiles, and sing to Your name." And again he says: "Rejoice, O Gentiles, with His people!" And again: "Praise the Lord, all you Gentiles! Laud Him, all you peoples!" (Romans 15:9-11)

Saying: "I will declare Your name to My brethren; in the midst of the assembly I will sing praise to You" (Hebrews 2:12).

Then a voice came from the throne, saying, "Praise our God, all you His servants and those who fear Him, both small and great!" (Revelation 19:5)

Let's take a look at some of the other Hebrew words that are used to describe acts of praise and worship:

1. *Chuwl*: to twist or twirl (in a circular or spiral manner); to dance.[42]

    This word is translated as *to dance* only two times in the Hebrew Scriptures. The first time is in Judges 21:21: "And see, and, behold, if the daughters of Shiloh come out to dance in dances, then come ye out of the vineyards, and catch you every man his wife of the daughters of Shiloh, and go to the land of Benjamin" (KJV). At this time, the tabernacle of the Lord was at Shiloh; if anyone wanted to inquire of the Lord, he was required to go there to do so. These women were dancing as part of the ceremonial worship of the Lord before the tabernacle of the Lord.

2. *Raqad*: to stamp, to spring about (wildly or for joy); to dance, to skip, to leap, to jump.[43]

    This word is used to describe the worship of King David when he danced wildly before the ark of the covenant and all the children of Israel (see 1 Chron. 15:29).

3. *Machowl*: a round dance.[44]

    This Hebrew word describes a choreographed round dance, which was used commonly in temple worship. The word appears first in Psalm 30:11: "You have turned for me my mourning into dancing; You have put off my sackcloth and clothed me with gladness."

This word is also used in a commanding sense in both Psalm 149 and 150.

4. *Karar*: to dance, to whirl.[45]

   Karar is only used twice and both times it appears in Second Samuel 6, describing the worship of King David before the glory of the Lord.

5. *Hallal*: to shine; to make a show, to boast; thus to be clamorously foolish; to rave; cause to celebrate, to praise.[46]

   This word is used more than 160 times in the Hebrew Scriptures and is translated *to praise* 117 of those times. This word is the source of a word which can be found in every language on earth: *Hallelujah*, which in Hebrew means "Let us praise Yah."

6. *Taqa'*: to strike one's hands together in praise or triumph.[47]

   Here we find another physical expression of praise: namely, the clapping of hands. Clapping hands in praise is actually only found four times in the Hebrew Scriptures; in Psalm 47:1, we see the clapping of hands as a command:

"Oh, clap your hands, all you peoples! Shout to God with the voice of triumph!" Again this verse demonstrates the close relationship between physical acts of worship and verbal acts of worship.

7. *Shachah*: to prostrate, worship, bow down, obeisance, reverence.[48]

     Shachah is usually translated *worship* (99 times in the Hebrew Scriptures); however, its root meaning is to prostrate in homage to God or royalty.

The most common word in the Hebrew language for praise and thanksgiving is the word *yadah*. It is used 114 times in the Hebrew Scriptures and occurs 70 times in the book of Psalms alone. The first time this word appears in the Old Testament is in Genesis 29:35. Leah, the unloved wife of Jacob, has had three children and is pregnant with the fourth. Each child she bears receives a name which is fitting for her situation. Leah is grateful for God's touch on her life and her ability to have children, which she believes will endear her to her husband, Jacob. The fourth child she names Judah, proclaiming, "Now I will praise the Lord." The word *praise* in this verse is the word *yadah*; the name Judah is a derivative of the same word.

Leah named each son she had according to her experience at

the time. Her first son she named Reuben, which means "see, a son," believing that because the Lord had looked upon her afflic-tion, her husband would love her. Her second son she named Simeon, which means "heard." She claimed, "Because the Lord has heard that I am unloved, He has therefore given me this son also" (Gen. 29:33). Again, Leah named Simeon, believing that her cir-cumstances would change and that she would be loved by her hus-band. Of course, we know that Jacob did not love his wife more because she bore him sons. Leah conceived again, and once again she named him out of her great desire to be loved by her husband. She said, "Now this time my husband will become attached to me, because I have borne him three sons" (Gen. 29:34). She called the third son Levi, which means "attached." Again, Leah conceived, yet with this child we see an important attitude change. Instead of nam-ing the boy based on her own desires, or in order to have a soulish need for affection fulfilled, Leah chose to praise God for what He had given her: namely, four sons! Leah called the fourth son Judah, which means praise. She proclaimed, "Now I will praise the Lord!" Finally Leah chose to worship the Lord in the midst of difficult cir-cumstances, being thankful for what He had accomplished for her already. Throughout her child-bearing time, Leah longed to be loved by her husband, Jacob. As soon as she turned from seeking her husband to praising the Lord, destiny began to work in her life and in the lives of her children.

I see a very important "God working with God" principle at work in this story. It was with this fourth child, Judah, that God did perhaps the greatest deeds among all the tribes of Israel. When praise was birthed, we see a significant paradigm shift among Leah's sons. When Leah chose to praise the Lord, God heard her and blessed this child above and beyond all of the others. Judah was not the firstborn; and in fact, in his lifetime, Judah did many things that would be considered false, impure, self-indulgent, and sinful. Judah slept with a prostitute (see Gen. 38:15-18), sold his brother as a slave (see Gen. 37:26-27), and did not train his sons in righteousness (see Gen. 38:6-10). In Judah's lifetime, we never really see the man called "Praise" actually praising the Lord. Instead, the story of his life is a litany of twisted and misplaced worship. Even in all this, God still chose Judah above his other brothers. Why? The reason lies in the praise. We have already firmly established that unless the Spirit within enables us to praise God it is impossible for us to offer anything to God that is acceptable. Only God can offer praise to God. When Leah praised the Lord, God recognized something of His own nature and character within her praise. God chose to exalt the one who was birthed in and through praise. As we will see from further study, it is through praise that victory is won, and it is through praise that the anointing flows. God will always exalt praise, and those who praise will be praised.

Anything that finds its origin in praise will attract praise.

After Judah makes many mistakes, we see a change in his

behavior, as he (Praise) intercedes for his brother Benjamin in Egypt. Judah/Praise willingly offers himself as a replacement for Benjamin so that Jacob will not be overcome with grief. The fact that Judah willingly intercedes for his brother gains him favor with Joseph and opens the door for reconciliation within the family of Israel. It is after this that Jacob calls his twelve sons together to bless them before he dies. The first three sons, namely, Reuben, Simeon, and Levi, Jacob does not speak blessing over. Jacob curses Reuben for defiling his father's bed by sleeping with his concubines, and Simeon and Levi he curses because they are men of rage and violence. Jacob refuses to allow his honor to be tied to them, and even prophesies that they will be scattered through the land of Israel. However, when Jacob comes to Judah, the tone of his words is completely altered:

> Judah, you are he whom your brothers shall praise; your hand shall be on the neck of your enemies; your father's children shall bow down before you. Judah is a lion's whelp; from the prey, my son, you have gone up. He bows down, he lies down as a lion; and as a lion, who shall rouse him? The scepter shall not depart from Judah, nor a lawgiver from between his feet, until Shiloh comes; and to Him shall be the obedience of the people. Binding his donkey to the vine, and his donkey's colt to the choice vine, he washed his garments in wine, and his clothes in the blood of

grapes. His eyes are darker than wine, and his teeth whiter than milk (Genesis 49:8-12).

This is a powerful word which Jacob spoke over his fourth son. Now remember, according to tradition, the eldest son was to receive a double portion from the father. In this case we see the fourth born son receiving the blessing. Jacob promised that Judah/Praise would receive praise from his brothers, and that the hand of Judah/Praise would be on the neck of his enemies. Jacob prophesies that Judah would be stronger than the rest—as strong as a lion, in fact. He also promises that Judah would father the great lawgivers and kings of Israel. All these blessings are promised to the one who was born through praise.

> **Praise always has its hand on the neck of its enemies.**

We can see these blessings develop throughout the books of First and Second Samuel, along with First and Second Chronicles. God develops a working relationship between the tribe of Judah and Himself, exalting Judah/Praise to a position of leadership, not only over the tribes of Israel but over many other countries as well. When God first sent Israel into Canaan to take the Promised Land, the Lord commanded that Judah lead the forces. Judah was the largest of all the tribes from the very beginning and had the largest inheritance within the land of Canaan (see Num. 1). Throughout all of the battles that the children of Israel fought, the tribe of Judah was the most consistently victorious. From the line of Judah came all the great kings: David, Solomon, Jehoshaphat, Hezekiah, Josiah, and Jesus.

In the lifetime of David, we see that God always gave him success over his enemies. Starting with the lions and the bears, continuing with Goliath and the Philistines, First Samuel makes it clear that David was victorious in hundreds of battles. What do you think the key to David's success was? David praised and worshiped God every day. David did not praise God according to his own resources, but according to what God had already planted within him. As he was faithful to release God's love back to God, God was faithful to deliver him from all his enemies. Once again praise had its hand on the neck of its enemies. The act of worshiping God is what set David above Saul. Saul was not a worshiper of God; in fact, he did not even claim the Lord as his God. Whenever he would speak to Samuel the prophet, he would always make a differentiation, saying, "The Lord *your* God" instead of "The Lord *my* God" or "The Lord *our* God." We know that because Saul rejected the word of the Lord, God rejected him, and chose for Himself a man after His own heart. God also makes a differentiation between those who love His Word and those who do not. We know that David loved and meditated on the Word of God from the very first psalm in the Book of Psalms:

> *Blessed is the man who walks not in the counsel of*
> *the ungodly, nor stands in the path of sinners, nor sits*

in the seat of the scornful; but his delight is in the law
of the Lord, and in His law he meditates day and
night (Psalm 1:1-2).

David's words make clear to us what a heart like God's is truly like. It is a heart that loves God's Word. A heart like God's sets itself toward God's precepts at all times. Another good example of this comes from Psalm 119. All but two of the 176 verses include something about God's law. As we discussed in the first chapter, studying the Word is one of the greatest forms of worship, taking into consideration the large amount of time it takes to examine God's Word carefully to glean what God has for you. The Bible says that God watches over His Word to perform it (see Jer. 1:12 NASB). David was demonstrating God's nature and character by lovingly examining God's Word with the same care that God takes as He watches over His Word. If we make God's Word our priority, then we will have the same priority as God. Of course, a heart that loves God's Word draws God's attention. It will draw His protection, His provision, and His promotion because God attracts God.

A heart like God's will attract God's
protection, provision, and promotion.

Throughout David's life the protection, the prosperity, and the promotion of God grew as David's revelation of God's love, mercy, and grace grew. The people around him could also see the favor of

God on his life. David was greatly loved by the people of Israel, and as the favor of God grew in David, so did his favor with leaders in his nation and others.

> So David went out wherever Saul sent him, and behaved wisely. And Saul set him over the men of war, and he was accepted in the sight of all the people and also in the sight of Saul's servants. Now it had happened as they were coming home, when David was returning from the slaughter of the Philistine, that the women had come out of all the cities of Israel, singing and dancing, to meet King Saul, with tambourines, with joy, and with musical instruments. So the women sang as they danced, and said: "Saul has slain his thousands, and David his ten thousands" (1 Samuel 18:5-7).

GOD WORKING WITH GOD PRODUCES FREEDOM

David, on the one hand, was accepted in the sight of all the people because he was acceptable in the sight of God. Promotion always comes to those who promote the agenda and purposes of God. God's Word is His written agenda for His people and the world, and when we promote His Word the Word will be promoted in us by God. Saul, on the other hand, because of his rejection of God's Word, experienced less and less favor, losing many battles and also losing the respect of the nation he led. Distressing spirits came and harassed Saul. Yet even Saul experienced the benefits of the "God working with God" relationship that flourished within David. As David worshiped the Lord, manifesting and releasing God's nature before God and toward God, Saul experienced the overflow of that love relationship and the distressing spirit would leave him. Equally, when David walked out of the room, the distressing spirits came back to harass Saul. Satan is attracted to satan's nature. When a person manifests hate, bitterness, rage, and unforgiveness, satan will have something of his own nature and character with which to work.

> *And so it was, whenever the spirit from God was upon Saul, that David would take a harp and play it with his hand. Then Saul would become refreshed and well, and the distressing spirit would depart from him* (1 Samuel 16:23).

As David chose to praise the Lord, his enemies would come and kneel at his feet. As David chose to praise the Lord, the evil spirits would flee. As David chose to praise the Lord, his foes were conquered. As David chose to praise the Lord, the Lord chose to praise and exalt Himself within David. At the same time, the people around him experienced the overflow of his love relationship with God; Saul experienced this, along with David's family. Because David chose to worship the Lord, he was able to defeat the giant

Goliath. The fruit of David defeating Goliath was exemption from paying taxes to the king. This is a powerful aspect to God's reciprocal nature: when we choose to worship and praise the Lord, God will choose to protect, provide for, and promote what He finds of Himself within us.

We see this principle demonstrated in the story of the wise men who came from the East to worship the new born King of the Jews. These men were not in covenant with God; they were not Jews, nor did they worship the God of the Jews. Yet they were able to build a "God working with God" connection through the avenue of worship and blessing that caused God's protection, provision, and promotion in their lives.

> Now after Jesus was born in Bethlehem of Judea in the days of Herod the king, behold, wise men from the East came to Jerusalem, saying, "Where is He who has been born King of the Jews? For we have seen His star in the East and have come to worship Him."…When they heard the king, they departed; and behold, the star which they had seen in the East went before them, till it came and stood over where the young Child was. When they saw the star, they rejoiced with exceedingly great joy. And when they had come into the house, they saw the young Child with Mary His mother, and fell down and worshiped Him. And when they had opened their treasures, they

presented gifts to Him: gold, frankincense, and myrrh.
Then, being divinely warned in a dream that they
should not return to Herod, they departed for their
own country another way (Matthew 2:1-2,9-12).

These men who were strangers and foreigners in the land of Israel were divinely warned in a dream that they should not return to Herod. God protected them and the baby Jesus thanks to the worship that they offered to the child. Worship opened the door in the spirit realm for God's favor to flow in those men's lives.

Worship opened the doorway for these men to hear God's voice. This is a powerful key to gaining accuracy in hearing the voice of God. When we worship the Lord we are speaking God's Word to God. We should expect that when we sow the Word into God we will reap a harvest of His voice in our lives. This was a spiritual promotion for the wise men. God's voice was only heard by those who were in covenant with God. As these men laid what was precious to them on the altar, God answered with a divine encounter that brought protection, provision, and promotion.

In this story we also see that when we release what is in our hand, we can expect God to release what is in His hand to us. The wise men were obviously rich and had great wealth. Their gifts were of great value, which showed their position in society. They were men of authority. They were obviously kings themselves. Yet by humbling themselves and offering a sacrifice of real value to the King of kings, they were merely returning to the Lord what belonged to Him already. We must realize that the gifts that these men laid at the feet of Jesus made Jesus' escape to Egypt possible. In effect, these men saved Jesus' life by financing a long road trip! We can see that what was of God—namely, the riches of the wise men—was given back to God—namely, Jesus and His family—to protect and preserve what was God's. God will always use what is of God to bring His perfect will to pass. And, we can see that because these men protected God, God protected them. They did not hold back what belonged to God, and God did not hold back in protecting, providing for, and promoting the wise men.

This is the explosive power of praise and worship. As we release what is of God's nature and character toward God and before God, we will see God's hand move on behalf of what originates in God.

THE DOORWAY TO DESTINY

Praise paves the way for God's power to move because it recognizes God's mighty hand in past triumphs, believes in God's faithfulness for the now, and sees God's vision for the future. Praise has clear vision to see that God's hand will move for God. Praise constantly reminds God of what He has already accomplished on behalf of His Word and His covenant people. Praise is a mirror back to God's mighty workings and consistent salvation. As a person praises God for past victories, he or she is creating a home for God to inhabit; an expectation begins to grow within concerning what

God will do in the future, giving God plenty of room to move as He pleases. God is attracted to praise and will move on behalf of those who praise Him. When we create a God-sized home by praising Him, we are making God's destiny for our lives the inevitable. Suppose a man builds a house specifically for himself—with the exact measurements, the right materials, the correct color options, the most expensive floors, and the most ornate fixtures—a house designed to meet his needs and please him. If he decides not to move in when it is finished, we would consider him ridiculous. So it would be if God did not inhabit the praise of His people. Praise creates an atmosphere where God's nature, character, and essence are the reigning factors. If God did not move in and take over, He would be denying Himself. God always possesses what belongs to Him, for, as we have already said, it is the Spirit of God within us that actually praises God, and not we ourselves. The purest praise of God comes from God and is directed toward God. We can expect that if we choose to release God's nature before and toward God by reminding Him of His mighty acts, God will inhabit our praise and take us as His prized possession. If you make room for God by praising Him, you can expect God's destiny to take hold of your life.

God's destiny always manifests in and through those who have yielded their mouths to praise.

As you study the Hebrew Scriptures, you will find that praise continued to have its hand on the neck of its enemies throughout Israel's history. If at any time Israel found itself in great trouble, and they chose to praise God instead of turning to human solutions, God always made a way for praise to have the victory. This again reminds us of God's reciprocal nature: God will only bring victory for God, and only those who are of God can praise God. We who praise God will be victorious through God. Let's look at another important story in the Hebrew Scriptures that demonstrates to us the power of praise.

> *Then the children of Israel arose and went up to the house of God to inquire of God. They said, "Which of us shall go up first to battle against the children of Benjamin?" The Lord said, "Judah first!"* (Judges 20:18)

The chapter that this verse comes out of tells a very powerful story. The story is of a Levite's concubine who was raped numerous times by a group of Benjaminite men, who then left her for dead. Through Benjamin's sin, the children of Israel gathered together to fight against them and purge the land of their great sin. This is a different sort of situation because the enemy is not attacking from without; instead, the enemy is within. The abuse was from brother to brother, an internal abuse of God's family. This kind of abuse still goes on today. When one part of the Body refuses to honor and respect another part of the Body, we see internal factions, strife, and envy begin to grow, causing disease and death within God's family.

Much of this can also be seen in the realm of touching God's anointed. We have given many examples of men and women in the Scripture who did not have a reverence for the chosen leader of God's people: Aaron and Miriam questioned God's delegated human authority. Another example is the sin of Achan in Joshua chapter 7, which caused 36 of his own fellow Israelites to be struck down and killed because Achan took the first fruits of the land that belonged to God. He and his whole family were stoned to death.

God chooses to deal with these kinds of situations in a different manner than if He was dealing with an outside attack by foreigners. God commands the people of Israel to go out against their brother Benjamin, putting Judah, or praise, in the front of the battle. Remember, that Judah, or praise, was the largest and strongest tribe of all the children of Israel. When God put praise in the front of the battle, He was making a statement about the internal struggle Israel was facing. I believe God was saying, "Internal strife and factions will only be dealt with when a heart of worship and honor is birthed in the people. When praise and honor correctly lead the people, victory is inevitable." God wants our level of praise and our honor for the anointing to soar high so that the jealousy, contention, and bitterness in the Body of Christ will be dealt with once and for all.

> Make a joyful shout to the Lord, all you lands! Serve
> the Lord with gladness; come before His presence
> with singing. Know that the Lord, He is God; it is He
> who has made us, and not we ourselves; we are His

people and the sheep of His pasture. Enter into His gates with thanksgiving, and into His courts with praise. Be thankful to Him, and bless His name. For the Lord is good; His mercy is everlasting, and His truth endures to all generations (Psalm 100).

The Hebrew word which we translate as *gates* is the word *sha'ar*. This word can refer to a fortified city gate with a tower. This gate was the entrance to the marketplace or the financial center of trade in a city. The legal courts of a city usually convened at the gates, and judgments, executions, and punishments were often carried out at the gates.[49] It is a powerful truth that God's children can enter His gates with thanksgiving. Thanksgiving makes available to us all that God is and all that God has. Thanksgiving is the key to God's marketplace: the supernatural flow of wealth toward God and from God toward His people. Thanksgiving is the key to God's wisdom, understanding, and knowledge. When you have a heart of thanksgiving, you will unlock God's desire to give you more of Himself. Philippians 4:6-7 says, "Be anxious for nothing, but in everything by prayer and supplication, with thanksgiving, let your requests be made known to God; and the peace of God, which surpasses all understanding, will guard your hearts and minds through Christ Jesus." Thanksgiving draws us into the strong tower of God's protective canopy. Thanksgiving covers us under His protective wing so that no harm may befall us. Remember that one of the key meanings of the word *yadah* is the aspect of thankfulness to the Lord. Part of praising God is being thankful for His goodness toward us.

We need to know without any doubt or wavering that it is God who created us. He is our sustaining factor, and all that we have originally proceeded out of God and must be returned to God through worship. This is where the revelation of God's goodness begins to take hold of us and manifest through us. When Abraham offered Isaac on the altar, he was giving his most precious possession to God (see Gen. 22). Abraham was laying down his destiny, his future, his inheritance on the altar before God. When Abraham chose to obey God, God chose to bless Abraham and his son Isaac forever.

> Then the Angel of the Lord called to Abraham a second time out of heaven, and said: "By Myself I have sworn, says the Lord, because you have done this thing, and have not withheld your son, your only son—blessing I will bless you, and multiplying I will multiply your descendents as the stars of the heaven and as the sand which is on the seashore; and your descendants shall possess the gate of their enemies. In your seed all the nations of the earth shall be blessed, because you have obeyed My voice" (Genesis 22:15-18).

God's promise to Abraham was that because Abraham was

faithful to worship the Lord and to give to God what was of God, namely the child of promise, God promised to give to Abraham's descendents the gates of their enemies. Isaac was a supernatural child, born out of due season for God's purposes. Abraham knew that Isaac belonged to God and not to his father. Abraham offered back to God what he had received from God. When we offer God what is of God, we are offering Him a sacrifice that is worthy of God. When we worship and praise God from God's resources, we will find that God will give us the gates of our enemies. Having looked at the meaning of this word (*sha'ar*), it should be clear that the gates can represent a place of justice, government, and wealth. As descendants of Abraham, we too inherit this promise; God's people can possess the strategic places of the enemy for the purposes of God. Once again we see that the destiny of praise is protection, prosperity, and promotion, for God only prospers what is of God.

THE EYES AND EARS OF JUDAH

Praise has the ability to see what is of God. The eyes that are focused on God can easily recognize what is of God in other people. That is why when David first became a leader in Israel, it was Judah who chose Him as king seven and a half years before he was anointed king over a unified Israel (see 2 Sam. 5:5). Judah was the first of the tribes to follow the one who had been chosen and anointed by the man of God, because praise and worship can recognize the voice of God.

*Those who are focused on praising God
can hear God's voice quickly and accurately
because they meditate on God's
Word frequently.*

It is interesting to me how closely praise is tied to the anointing. This makes perfect sense when we recognize that God's power flows in direct response to God's Word. Jesus descended from King David and from the line of Judah. Praise is us speaking forth the truth of God toward God and before God. If our practice is to praise the Lord by reminding Him of His Word and the mighty signs and wonders He has done in our lives, we should expect that God's anointing is going to flow through us. The destiny of praise is power, for it is only those who praise God who are given access to His power. The secrets of God's supernatural strength are revealed to those who worship God in spirit and truth.

Those who are strong in the Spirit are able to recognize God's delegated authority more quickly than those who are not. When a person spends time in the presence of God, studying the Word, praying, and worshiping the Lord, it will become obvious because of their ability to see God and recognize true spiritual authority. People who spend time loving the Lord are also the ones to whom God will send spiritual authority. These people seek out authority instead of running away from it, because they are drawn to people who know more about God than they do. People who spend time loving on God are hungry to receive the Word of God from other people. A good example of this is found in Acts chapter 16:

> *And on the Sabbath day we went out of the city to the riverside, where prayer was customarily made; and we sat down and spoke to the women who met there. Now a certain woman named Lydia heard us. She was a seller of purple from the city of Thyatira, who worshiped God. The Lord opened her heart to heed the things spoken by Paul* (Acts 16:13-14).

Do you see that Lydia was a worshiper of God already? That means she spent considerable amount of time in the presence of the Lord. When a greater authority than herself showed up at her prayer meeting, she was not proud toward Paul or arrogant: instead, she was humble and listened to what he had to say. In the end she decided to become his disciple, and even blessed Paul and Silas financially by inviting them to stay in her house. Through the avenue of praise and worship, Lydia's heart was prepared to receive God's delegated authority into her heart, life, and home.

In Acts chapter 18 we see another example of this. At first, as was his custom, Paul went to preach in the synagogue on the Sabbath. As a result of religious bondage, however, the people in the synagogue would not receive what Paul had to say to them. They despised his freedom in Christ and rejected the Word of the Lord, as Saul had before them. Paul told them, "Your blood be upon your own heads; I am clean. From now on I will go to the Gentiles" (Acts 18:6). Let's look at the next verse: "And he departed from there and entered the house of a certain man named Justus, one who worshiped God, whose house was next door to the synagogue" (Acts 18:7).

Again we see a Gentile believer, one who worshiped God, but was not involved with the traditions of the Jews. Not only was he a Gentile, but he also lived right next door to the synagogue. This was definitely a slap in the face of the religious Jews who would not receive the Word of God from Paul. All that this man had going for him was that he was a worshiper of God. Yet that was enough for Paul. This man attracted apostolic attention from the man who wrote two-thirds of the New Testament, all based on the fact that he was a worshiper of God, nothing more, nothing less.

Those who worship God should be able to tell what is of God and what is not. Another good example of a person who worshiped the Lord and could recognize spiritual authority is found in Matthew chapter 8:

> When He had come down from the mountain, great multitudes followed Him. And behold, a leper came and worshiped Him, saying, "Lord, if You are willing, You can make me clean." Then Jesus put out His hand and touched him, saying, "I am willing; be cleansed." Immediately his leprosy was cleansed (Matthew 8:1-3).

The Scripture says that the leper fell down and worshiped Jesus. This man had a disease that caused anyone who touched him to be considered unclean. Leprosy was connected to unclean spirits. The man turned to Jesus and said, "If it is your will, Lord." Jesus could have pointed out the man's sins. He could have questioned the man. But He did not. Jesus based His response not on the fact that the leper was a good man, but on the fact that the man had come and worshiped Jesus. The leper recognized that Jesus was God and deserving of worship. That was enough for Jesus, and the man was immediately cleansed. When God saw His nature and character proceed out of the man, whether he was a leper or not, He responded and drove that sickness far away.

When the thief hung on the cross next to Jesus, all the he had to say was "Lord." When the man called Jesus Lord, he was recognizing who Jesus really was. He could look at a man who was hanging on a cross, beaten black and blue, his hair and beard ripped out, his body shredded from a cat-of-nine-tails, and that thief could still see God. This is so important. Can we look at church leadership, even though they have been beaten up by all kinds of circumstances and troubles, even though they make mistakes, can we look at them and still see the call, the vision, the purposes of God in their lives? If the thief who knew nothing about the Lord could look at Jesus and see God, we as God's children, born again and filled with God's Spirit, have no excuse for not seeing God in the people around us. We must choose to look for what is of God in our pastors and leaders. We must choose to respect, honor, and venerate what is of God in our spouses. We must choose to allow the Spirit of God within us to rise up in recognition of God in others; if we do not, we will end up missing those who are called to be Davids and Solomons, Hezekiahs, Jehoshaphats, and Josiahs. It's our choice.

When the thief on the cross recognized that Jesus was Lord, he was claiming Jesus as the owner of his life. He was saying, "You are the Master. You are the Landlord." Do you know that God knows how to save what is of God? God will always claim what belongs to Him. For this reason the thief was saved, because Jesus claimed him as His own. You may be struggling with many things. You may even have demonic spirits harassing you. But I promise that if you will come to the altar and fall down on your face and worship the true and living God, you will be saved, no matter what you are struggling with. God has never once denied a person who has worshiped Him, for worship can only come out of God's nature and character. In order for a person to worship, there must be something of God within that person, and God will always save God.

JUDAH'S DESTINY IS VICTORY

I want to go back and revisit the story of Jehoshaphat once more. This is a key event to understanding God's reciprocal nature concerning praise. Remember that First Corinthians 2:9 tells us that "eye has not seen, nor ear heard, nor have entered into the heart of man the things which God has prepared for those who love Him." Romans 8:28 tells us that "all things work together for good to those who love God…who are the called according to His purpose." You see, those who manifest the nature of God before God and toward God are the ones who will reap a harvest of God. God's love has been shed abroad in our hearts for the purpose of manifesting it back to God and sowing it as seed into other people's hearts. Let's look at a "God working with God" pattern that God has set up for us to follow:

> So they rose early in the morning and went out into the Wilderness of Tekoa; and as they went out, Jehoshaphat stood and said, "Hear me, O Judah and you inhabitants of Jerusalem: Believe in the Lord your God, and you shall be established; believe His prophets, and you shall prosper" (2 Chronicles 20:20).

The first step laid down for us in this story is to believe God. What a simple yet powerful concept: Hebrews 11:6 tells us that "without faith it is impossible to please God, for he who comes to God must believe that He is, and that He is a rewarder of those who diligently seek Him." It is very important that when you worship God you believe that He is powerful. You must believe that God is able to perform His Word. Before you can experience the reward, for we know that He is a rewarder of those who diligently seek Him, you must believe that He is everything that He says He is. You must believe that the all-knowing, all-powerful, majestic One is in you and is working His will and destiny through you. You must accept and receive the inner workings of the Holy Spirit before you will see the true delivering power of praise birthed through you.

The second principle laid out in the story is to believe God's prophets. This may seem simple to you, but it brings us back to a very old and common issue among God's children: rebellion. It may be easy for you to say, "Yes, I believe God's Word," or "Yes, I listen to the Holy Spirit," yet what happens when God sends His word by a messenger? What happens when His word is correction? Rebellion can hinder us more than anything else from entering into the fullness of God's destiny and victory. At times God sends His word through other people to test the perception of love that is being birthed on the inside of us. God knows that the God in us will always recognize the God in another person. God knows that praise can perceive God's chosen vessel. Our response to the man or woman of God will be a manifestation of where we are in praise and worship. Is God's love ruling and reigning through us? Then it should not be a problem to receive what is of God in another person who is sent from God. Again we see this principle in the people of Israel's avid acceptance of David as their king: God's chosen people were able to see what was of God in God's chosen king. Those who were not of God, those who did not worship God or claim God as their own, could not see what God saw in David. They could not see the destiny of praise operating in his life.

> *And when he had consulted with the people, he*
> *appointed those who should sing to the Lord, and*

who should praise the beauty of holiness, as they went out before the army and were saying: "Praise the Lord, for His mercy endures forever" (2 Chronicles 20:21).

Acceptable praise will always flow out of the place of holiness.

The third principle to gaining the victory through praise lies in holiness. Notice from this verse that acceptable praise will always flow out of the place of holiness. As we discussed in Chapter Five, the people of Israel are bringing God in remembrance of His covenant. They are proclaiming to God, "You are a covenant-keeping God. You always perform Your Word." Jehoshaphat knew that one of the keys to God's covenant was walking in holiness. God had commanded them to "be holy; for I am holy" (Lev. 11:44). Jehoshaphat knew that the worship that would be acceptable and pleasing to the Lord had to flow from the place of God's holiness. Once again, He was bringing God in remembrance of God.

We can see the results from the principles of belief, submission to God's Word, and holiness: God looked down at the children of Israel and saw Himself. Once again praise opened the door for deliverance to enter in. The children of Israel were delivered from their enemies, and praise had the victory over those who came against it. God caused confusion to come into the enemy's camp so that they destroyed each other instead of destroying Israel. Instead of the enemy working together to rout God's children, the enemy was divided against itself. Praise had its hand on the neck of its enemies and was victorious. When we praise God, we can expect God to take care of the enemy, remove the opposition, and silence the spiritual warfare that is coming against us.

We need to realize that praise is a trumpet blast in the ears of God—praise is the quickest way to get God's attention, because it centers on His nature and character. God is so attracted to what He finds of Himself in our praise and adoration of Him, it is inevitable that He will move heaven and earth on our behalf. He will split the heavens and come down to deliver us from the hand of our enemies. Praise will always have the victory over its enemies. Praise will experience the protection, the prosperity, and the promotion of God, and praise will attract more praise. Remember that David had favor with everyone he came in contact with, and his life was full of praise and worship to the Most High God. As we release God's nature before God and toward God, God is going to make a way for His nature and character to flourish in the earth, no matter what it takes to make it happen. God will be faithful to work with God in us and bring the destiny of God to pass in our lives, as we let praise rule and reign in our mouths.

GWWG LOVE AND WORSHIP:

MEDITATIONS OF THE HEART

- Anything that finds its origin in praise will attract praise.

- Praise always has its hand on the neck of its enemies.

- A heart like God's will attract God's protection, provision, and promotion.

- God's destiny always manifests in and through those who have yielded their mouths to praise.

- Those who are focused on praising God can hear God's voice quickly and accurately because they meditate on God's Word frequently.

- Acceptable praise will always flow out of the place of holiness.

CHAPTER SEVEN

YOU SHALL LOVE THE LORD YOUR GOD

THE JUDGMENTS OF GOD

Praise the Lord! Sing to the Lord a new song, and His praise in the assembly of the saints. Let Israel rejoice in their Maker; Let the children of Zion be joyful in their King. Let them praise His name with the dance; let them sing praises to Him with the timbrel and harp. For the Lord takes pleasure in His people; He will beautify the humble with salvation. Let the saints be joyful in glory; let them sing aloud on their beds. Let the high praises of God be in their

*mouth, and a two-edged sword in their hand, to exe-
cute vengeance on the nations, and punishments on
the peoples; to bind their kings with chains, and their
nobles with fetters of iron; to execute on them the
written judgment—this honor have all His saints.
Praise the Lord!* (Psalm 149)

As I read this chapter, I can feel the power of God surging through the words. We are commanded by God to praise Him, to sing new songs to Him, to make a joyful noise, to dance, to clap, to play instruments. God is not asking us to come before Him with singing; He is commanding us to come before Him with singing! The question lies with us: Will we? Will we worship the Lord our God with all of our hearts? Will we praise Him for His mighty deeds? Will we worship Him in spirit and truth, offering Him the worship that He deserves? Will we manifest and release God's nature and character before God and toward God in order to attract God in our lives? The choice lies with us. We must choose to allow God's love to rule and reign in our hearts so that the worship we offer to God comes out of the love of God, and not out of human empathy. We must allow the Spirit of God within us to worship the Father God in Heaven, letting God work with His nature and character within us. We must allow God to develop a "God working with God" synergy in our worship so that we can go from glory to glory, going ever deeper into the things of God.

Psalm 149 makes it clear that the pure praise and worship of

God's people will lead them into victory over every enemy that stands in their way. Worship has an incredible ability to divide between what is of the flesh and what is of the spirit. In the above verses you will find five different judgments that those who worship God in spirit and truth will exact upon the enemies of God. In fact the last verse tells us that it is an honor that God gives to His saints. Again I see a powerful "God working with God" synergy in these verses: those who worship God by releasing God's nature and character before and toward God will experience God's victory and will become partakers of His divine judgments. It is powerful to see, even in small ways, how God's judgments begin to move during a worship service. People will come in as visitors and sit in the back row. They are skeptical and judgmental, not judging according to the Spirit of God. As the worship service begins, the manifestation of God's nature and character begins to work on their hearts. The preacher has not even stepped up to the pulpit to preach, and already the people are cut to the quick with conviction. The judgments of God are already being administered through the worship music, drawing the people to repentance and change. One of the greatest products of true worship is the conviction of the Holy Spirit. Those who are being convicted look at the people around them; they see the victorious saints of God worshiping with all of their hearts and ask themselves, "Do I really love God?" Seeing the true love of God demonstrated to them by other believers has a way of bringing them to a place of hunger again.

Worship is not that complicated. The only question is, "Do you love Jesus?" If you love Jesus, then worshiping Him in spirit and truth and offering to God His own nature and character on the altar will not be a problem for you. Every time you step into the place of worship, God will take you to another place in Him where you will learn how to give Him even more than you already have. Releasing God's Spirit through our words is the greatest key to moving into higher realms of praise. It takes the Holy Spirit quickening our words in order to go from one level of glory to another. It takes God in your mouth in order to get a God response. Our songs must go beyond pretty melodies and great instrumentals; they must have the breath of God upon them in order to reach God's ears and touch God's heart. And, hopefully, this is our goal: to worship God in spirit and truth.

> *For we are the circumcision, who worship God in the Spirit, rejoice in Christ Jesus, and have no confidence in the flesh* (Philippians 3:3).

Your flesh cannot exalt God; in fact, it has no desire to! It is only when the Spirit of God within you takes over that you can truly worship God. When the Spirit of God takes control, you might want to dance like David before the glory of the Lord. David was excited about God, so excited that he lost sight of his position. One thing I have noticed about the presence of the Lord is that it humbles those who are exalted and exalts those who are humble. You see, when David danced with all his might before God, he was worshiping God from the purity of his heart, as he had when he watched over the sheep in Bethlehem. He was unashamed and became undignified, because He was only concerned about pleasing the heart of his Father. He was no longer acting as the great king of Israel—he was behaving as God's little boy, God's child. It is important that we get free in worship so that we can dance before God as His dear little children.

Let's look at one more Hebrew word concerning worship: *barak*.[50] This word means to bless God; it also means to kneel down before God. *Barak* appears over 300 times in the Hebrew Scriptures. It is used to describe people blessing God and people blessing other people. The most significant use of the word *barak* is in its first and second appearances in Genesis chapter 1. First, God speaks blessing over the animals and commands them to be fruitful and multiply. Then God speaks blessing over Adam in a similar way, but adds to it that he must take dominion and subdue the earth. God thereby sets a precedent, as we have already discussed, as the author of blessing; God has written blessing in our hearts, and our ability to bless flows out of the blessing we have received from God. The word *barak* itself implies that God is the Beginner or Author of all blessing, and that it is actually the Holy Spirit within us who blesses God through us. Dr. Myles Munroe's observations on this word shed more light on the "God working with God" synergy that must be present in worship:

> *Barak* therefore carries with it a sense of hushed
> expectancy and often comes when the Holy Spirit

begins to minister, filling the praise that has been offered. In this sense, *barak* is the beginning of God's response in worship.[51]

It is the Spirit of God within us who is able to bless God in a manner that is fitting. Just as the Word says, it is fitting for the upright to give praise to God; we know that the only One who is truly upright is the Lord Himself. It is His Spirit within us who enables us to worship God according to the Spirit. For only God can worship God in spirit and truth. The blessing of God can only proceed out of the Holy Spirit of God. God wants us to learn how to respond to God by blessing out of the resources of God's blessing within us. When God created Adam, He spoke blessing over him. When He brought Noah through the flood, He spoke blessing over him. When God brought Abraham out of his country, God promised to bless him and to give him an inheritance. God initiated blessing in all three cases, as He did with multitudes of His people throughout the ages. He has blessed us in many ways. For example, when we release the healing anointing to touch others' lives, we are also releasing the blessings of God upon people's lives, which brings wholeness, healing, and deliverance. In return, a harvest of blessings is reaped. God is not only in expectation that we will return blessing to God out of the resources of blessing that God has given us access to through His Holy Spirit, God is also in expectation that He will receive the same kind of love back from us that He has given to us.

Of course, God's expectation is based in God. God knows that whatever He sows, He will reap back one hundredfold. God is in expectation that the seed of His Son, which He sowed in love, will reap Him a harvest of millions of sons who will lay down their lives for Him, just as Jesus did. He has sown Himself into us, and God is believing that He will reap a harvest of Himself out of us.

We need to recognize that when we worship God we are going to attract what is of God and repel the demonic forces. When Jesus was tempted by the devil after he had been fasting for 40 days and nights, Jesus continually replied with the Word of God. However, when Jesus said to satan, "Away with you, Satan! For it is written, 'You shall worship the Lord your God, and Him only shall you serve,'" the Bible tells us that satan immediately left Jesus, and the angels came and ministered to Him (Matt. 4:10-11). Worship attracts the angelic forces and silences spiritual warfare. If you are coming under attack, the quickest way to silence the voice of the enemy is to simply lift your hands to worship the Lord. For God hears Himself when we worship Him in spirit and truth, and God will answer Himself and deliver us from the enemy.

GOD HAS EARS FOR GOD

Brothers and sisters, the truth lies in the power of the "God working with God" synergy. The most important thing you must glean from this book is that God in Heaven desires, even jealously yearns for, the God in you. When we worship God we must choose to manifest what is of God before God so that we will be a mirror of

God. The Bible makes it clear that God hears those who worship God and do His will (see John 9:31). In John chapter 9, we see the story of the blind man who was healed by Jesus. This is a very important story to understand fully the concept of God working with God. Let us look at the first five verses of chapter 9:

> Now as Jesus passed by, He saw a man who was blind from birth. And His disciples asked Him, saying, "Rabbi, who sinned, this man or his parents, that he was born blind?" Jesus answered, "Neither this man nor his parents sinned, but that the works of God should be revealed in him. I must work the works of Him who sent Me while it is day; the night is coming when no one can work. As long as I am in the world, I am the light of the world" (John 9:1-5).

Jesus made it clear to His disciples that what was important was not whether the man or his parents sinned. Jesus pointed out to the disciples that God had chosen the man to reveal the works of God in and through. When Jesus looked at the blind man, He saw what was of God within that man that God wanted to bring forth. Jesus told His disciples that He *must* work the works of God. Jesus was bound by the principle of "God working with God" to work with what was of God's nature and character in the blind man. As you will see in the following verses, it was worship that attracted Jesus to the man.

So they again called the man who was blind, and said to him, "Give God the glory! We know that this Man is a sinner." He answered and said, "Whether He is a sinner or not I do not know. One thing I do know: that though I was blind, now I see.... Now we know that God does not hear sinners; but if anyone is a worshiper of God and does His will, He hears him. Since the world began it has been unheard of that anyone opened the eyes of one who was born blind. If this Man were not from God, He could do nothing" (John 9:24-25,31-33).

The man who was born blind was called before the Sanhedrin and questioned about his miracle. They continued to berate and criticize both him and Jesus. Finally, the man who had been healed said to them, "Now we know that God does not hear sinners; but if anyone is a worshiper of God and does His will, He hears him." The man was claiming that while he was blind he had continued to worship God. God had something to work with within the man who was born blind: His own nature and character, a heart of love, a heart like God's.

The blind man made it clear why he received his sight: it was because he worshiped God. When we love God, we are releasing God's nature and character back to God. We are giving to God the worship that He truly deserves; He deserves to receive what is of God. Jesus was attracted to this man because He could see a heart like God's within him. Jesus recognized what was of God in the man who was born blind, and worked the works of God based on a "God working with God" principle. In verse 4, Jesus tells His disciples, "I must work the works of Him who sent Me...." Jesus is basically telling them, "What is of God in Me is programmed to work with the God in this man and in every person. God must work with God."

When we manifest and release God's nature and character before and toward God, we can expect that God will hear us, because God is in the habit of keeping His Word and honoring His obligations. God has obligated Himself to honor every word that He has spoken, and He has promised us that if we will draw near to God, then He will draw near to us. If we will love God and worship Him from a heart like God's, God is going to shake the prisons and set the captives free. God will use the "God working with God" synergy flowing out of our lives to touch the nations and release those who are in bondage to sin and death. There are times when I have preached this subject I have realized that to bring clarity to what I am saying, I have to be dead to self and alive to God, and that only God and what God would have to say needs to be seen and heard. In this revelation, great power has manifested in mighty signs and wonders.

As God's nature and character within us touches God in Heaven, there will be a multiplication that takes place, drawing others into a powerful "God working with God" relationship. We can see this principle with any common seed; one seed has the power to produce thousands of others just like it. It is the same when we worship God from a heart like God's, allowing God's nature to manifest toward God. God's love in us will produce God's love in others, setting them free to worship God from a heart like God's.

Wherever God finds Himself He sets Himself free. A good example of this is found in chapter 16 of the Book of Acts: Paul and Silas had been beaten severely and thrown into jail. Even though Paul and Silas were Roman citizens, they were beaten without a trial and thrown into prison. Though their circumstances looked very grim, Paul and Silas chose to worship God in the midst of their trouble. Even while they were chained up in prison, they sang songs to the Lord and praised His name.

> But at midnight Paul and Silas were praying and singing hymns to God, and the prisoners were listening to them. Suddenly there was a great earthquake, so that the foundations of the prison were shaken; and immediately all the doors were opened and everyone's chains were loosed (Acts 16:25-26).

This story demonstrates the power that one worshiper of God can have on the people around him or her. Jesus told the disciples that where two or three are gathered in His name, He is there in the midst of them (see Matt. 18:20). If I am in the Name and you are in the Name, we have agreement in God. If we so choose, we can worship the Lord until the bondages and chains that bind our families and friends fall right off. The overflow of the love relationship between God in Heaven and God in Paul and Silas caused the chains of all the prisoners to be loosed. This should be a common occurrence in our churches. I have experienced meetings where one person gets healed, and because of it, other sick people's healings are unlocked and released. In our worship services, when prophetic worship is released, we have seen many visitors touched by the presence of God that is released through prophetic worship.

When a person comes in who is bound with sin and by the power of the enemy, our worship of God should set them free to worship freely as well. However, every person must realize that it is his or her job to remain free once he or she leaves the church building. Experiencing the overflow of another person's intimate relationship with God may set you free, but the only thing that will keep you free is God within you being intimate with God in Heaven. Every believer must learn to release God's nature and character before and toward God to maintain God's voice, presence, and power in his or her own life.

THE DIVINE ATTRACTION REVEALED

I am convinced that as you have read the pages of this book, God has greatly moved in your heart to bring you to a greater understanding of the "God working with God" synergy in worship. Worship is releasing God's character and nature before God and toward God. God will inevitably be attracted to His nature and character manifesting out of you. As you worship the Lord in spirit (who is God) and truth (who is God), I believe you will see amazing breakthroughs take place in your life, as God brings protection, provision, and promotion to Himself within you. It is what is of God's nature and character within you that God will cause to grow and multiply in amazing ways as you manifest more and more of who He is.

It is your turn now. Manifest and release God's nature and character before and toward God so that God can use the overflow of your love relationship to touch your community and your world. Allow God's Spirit within you to rise up and touch God in Heaven. Turn your home, your car, and your workplace into the sanctuary of the Lord, where God's voice, presence, and power are always welcome and at home. Turn your life into a living sacrifice, holy and acceptable, which is your reasonable worship. Give God what is of God, and watch God bring protection, prosperity, and promotion into your life as you experience the revelation that God in Heaven is working with God in you!

ENDNOTES

1. James Strong, *The New Strong's Expanded Exhaustive Concordance of the Bible: Strong's Expanded Greek Dictionary of the New Testament* (Nashville, TN: Thomas Nelson Publishers, 2001), 212.

2. Doug Wheeler, *For the Love of God: A Conceptual Study of the Love of God* (Bossier City, LA: Mended Wings Ministries, Inc., 1996), 4.

3. James Strong, *The New Strong's Expanded Exhaustive Concordance of the Bible: Strong's Expanded Hebrew and Aramaic Dictionary* (Nashville, TN: Thomas Nelson Publishers, 2001), 204.

4. Please read and listen to the author's book and CD series *God in Your Mouth*, available at www.swordministries.org.

5. For more information on this subject, please visit us at www.swordministries.org and order the CD series *The Timeless Eternal Realm*.

6. Strong, *Greek Dictionary*, 141.

7. Strong, *Greek Dictionary*, 71-72.

8. LaMar Boschman, *A Heart of Worship* (Orlando, FL: Charisma House, 1994), 21.

9. Please read and listen to *God Working With God: Spirit to Spirit*, available at www.swordministries.org.

10. Boschman, *A Heart of Worship*, 21.

11. Judson Cornwall, *Let Us Praise* (Plainfield, NJ: Logos International, 1973), 28.

12. Strong, *Greek Dictionary*, 270.

13. Boschman, *A Heart of Worship*, 21.

14. Wheeler, *For the Love of God*, 5.

15. Wheeler, *For the Love of God*, 5.

16. Please listen to the author's series *Ephesians: Ministering From the Throne* available at www.swordministries.org.

17. For more information, please read *Presenting a Yielded Will*, and please listen to *The Setting of a Bone*, both available at www.swordministries.org.

18. For more information, please listen to the author's CD series *Can You See What God Is Saying?* available at www .swordministries.org.

19. Strong, *Greek Dictionary*, 202.

20. Strong, *Greek Dictionary*, 60-61.

21. Strong, *Hebrew and Aramaic Dictionary*, 108.

22. Strong, *Hebrew and Aramaic Dictionary*, 139.

23. Strong, *Hebrew and Aramaic Dictionary*, 6.

24. Strong, *Greek Dictionary*, 135.

25. Strong, *Hebrew and Aramaic Dictionary*, 282.

26. Strong, *Hebrew and Aramaic Dictionary*, 21.

27. Boschman, *A Heart of Worship*, 23.

28. Strong, *Greek Dictionary*, 212.

29. Strong, *Greek Dictionary*, 214.

30. Strong, *Hebrew and Aramaic Dictionary*, 177.

31. Strong, *Hebrew and Aramaic Dictionary*, 39.

32. Strong, *Hebrew and Aramaic Dictionary*, 287.

33. Strong, *Hebrew and Aramaic Dictionary*, 282.

34. For more information on the glory of God, please read the author's book and listen to his CD series *The Weightiness of God*.

35. Please listen to the author's CD series *The Setting of a Bone* for more information.

36. For more information on this subject, please see the author's book *God Working With God*, available online at www.swordministries.org.

37. Strong, *Hebrew and Aramaic Dictionary*, 93.

38. For more information on this subject, please see Judson Cornwall's powerful book *Let Us Praise*.

39. Cornwall, *Let Us Praise*, 50.

40. Cornwall, *Let Us Praise*, 50.

41. Strong, *Hebrew and Aramaic Dictionary*, 107.

42. Strong, *Hebrew and Aramaic Dictionary*, 81-82.

43. Strong, *Hebrew and Aramaic Dictionary*, 267.

44. Strong, *Hebrew and Aramaic Dictionary*, 153.

45. Strong, *Hebrew and Aramaic Dictionary*, 137.

46. Strong, *Hebrew and Aramaic Dictionary*, 69.

47. Strong, *Hebrew and Aramaic Dictionary*, 301.

48. Strong, *Hebrew and Aramaic Dictionary*, 275.

49. Strong, *Hebrew and Aramaic Dictionary*, 287-288.

50. Strong, *Hebrew and Aramaic Dictionary*, 46-47.

51. Dr. Myles Munroe, *The Purpose and Power of Praise and Worship* (Shippensburg, PA: Destiny Image Publishers, Inc., 2000), 118.